Praise for the "Kids Love" Guidebook travel series
On-Air Personality Comments (Television Interviews)

"The great thing about these books is that your whole family actually lives these adventures" – (**WKRC-TV**, Cincinnati)

"Very helpful to lots of families when the kids say, I bored...and I don't want to go to same places again!" – (**WISH-TV**, Indianapolis)

"Dividing the state into many sections, the book has something for everyone...everywhere." – (**WLVT-TV**, Pennsylvania)

"These authors know first-hand that it's important to find hands-on activities that engage your children..." (**WBNS-TV**, Columbus)

"You spent more than 1000 hours doing this research for us, that's really great – we just have to pick up the book and it's done..."
(**WTVR-TV**, Richmond)

"A family that's a great source for travel ideas..."
(**WBRA-TV**, Roanoke)

"What a great idea...this book needed to be done a long time ago!"
(**WKYT-TV**, Lexington)

"A fabulous idea...places to travel that your kids will enjoy"
(**WOOD-TV**, Grand Rapids)

"The Zavatskys call it a dream come true, running their own business while keeping the family together. Their goal, encourage other parents to create special family travel memories." - (**WLVT-TV**, Pennsylvania)

"It's a wonderful book, and as someone who has been to a lot of these places...you hit it right on the money!" – (**WKRC-TV**, Cincinnati)

Praise for the "Kids Love" Guidebook travel series
Customer Comments (actual letters on file)

"I wanted to tell you how helpful all your books have been to my family of 6. I rarely find books that cater to families with kids. I have your Indiana, Ohio, Kentucky, Michigan, and Pennsylvania books. I don't want to miss any of the new books that come out. Keep up the great ideas. The books are fantastic. I have shown them to tons of my friends. They love them, too." – H.M.

"I bought the Ohio and Indiana books yesterday and what a blessing these are for us!!! We love taking our grandsons on Grammie & Papaw trips thru the year and these books are making it soooo much easier to plan. The info is complete and full of ideas. Even the layout of the book is easy to follow...I just wanted to thank you for all your work in developing these books for us..." – G.K

"I have purchased your book. My grandchildren and I have gone to many of the places listed in your book. They mark them off as we visit them. We are looking forward to seeing many more. It is their favorite thing to look at book when they come over and find new places to explore. Thank you for publishing this book!" - B.A.

"At a retail price of under $15.00, any of the books would be well worth buying even for a one-time only vacation trip. Until now, when the opportunity arose for a day or weekend trip with the kids I was often at a loss to pick a destination that I could be sure was convenient, educational, child-friendly, and above all, fun. Now I have a new problem: How in the world will we ever be able to see and do all the great ideas listed in this book? I'd better get started planning our next trip right away. At least I won't have to worry about where we're going or what to do when we get there!" – VA Homeschool Newsletter

"My family and I used this book this summer to explore Ohio! We lived here nearly our entire life and yet over half the book we never knew existed. These people really know what kids love! Highly recommended for all parents, grandparents, etc." – Barnes and Noble website reviewer

KIDS ♥ LOVE INDIANA

A Parent's Guide to Exploring
Fun Places in Indiana
With Children...Year Round!

George & Michele Zavatsky

Dedicated to the Families of Indiana

ISBN-13: 978-0972685443
ISBN-10: 0-972685448

TABLE OF CONTENTS

(Amusements, Animals & Farms, Museums, Outdoors, State History, Tours, etc.)

State Map

(With Major Routes and Cities Marked)

Chapter Area Map

CITY INDEX (*Listed by City & Area*)

CITY INDEX (*Listed by City & Area*)

Cities appearing in *italics* occur
only in the Seasonal Chapter

Acknowledgements

We are most thankful to be blessed with our parents, Barbara (Darrall) Callahan & George and Catherine Zavatsky who help us every way they can – researching, proofing and babysitting. More importantly, they are great sounding boards and offer unconditional support. So many places around Indiana remind us of family vacations years ago…

We also want to express our thanks to the many Convention & Visitor Bureaus' staff for providing the attention to detail that helps to complete a project. We felt very welcome during our travels in Indiana and would be proud to call it home!

Our own kids, Jenny and Daniel, were delightful and fun children during our trips across the state. What a joy it is to be their parents…we couldn't do it without them as our "kid-testers"!

We both sincerely thank each other – our partnership has created an even greater business/personal "marriage" with lots of exciting moments, laughs, and new adventures in life woven throughout. Above all, we praise the Lord for His so many blessings through the last few years.

We think Indiana is a wonderful, friendly area of the country with more activities than you could imagine. Our sincere wish is that this book will help everyone "fall in love" with Indiana.

In a Hundred Years...

It will not matter, The size of my bank account...
The kind of house that I lived in, the kind of car that I drove...
But what will matter is...
That the world may be different
Because I was important in the life of a child.
- *author unknown*

HOW TO USE THIS BOOK

If you are excited about discovering Indiana, this is the book for you and your family! We've spent over a thousand hours doing all the scouting, collecting and compiling (*and most often visiting!*) so that you could spend less time searching and more time having fun.

Here are a few hints to make your adventures run smoothly:

❑   Consider the **child's age** before deciding to take a visit.

❑   Know **directions** and parking. Call ahead (or visit the company's website) if you have questions *and* bring this book. Also, don't forget your camera! *(please honor rules regarding use).*

❑   **Estimate the duration** of the trip. Bring small surprises (favorite juice boxes) travel books, and toys.

❑   Call ahead for **reservations** or details, if necessary.

❑   Most listings are **closed major holidays** unless noted.

❑   Make a **family "treasure chest"**. Decorate a big box or use an old popcorn tin. Store memorabilia from a fun outing, journals, pictures, brochures and souvenirs. Once a year, look through the "treasure chest" and reminisce. "Kids Love Travel Memories!" is an excellent travel journal & scrapbook that your family can create. *(See the order form in back of this book).*

❑   Plan **picnics** along the way. Many State History sites and state parks are scattered throughout Indiana. Allow time for a rural /scenic route to take advantage of these free picnic facilities.

❑   Some activities, especially tours, require **groups** of 10 or more. To participate, you may either ask to be part of another tour group or get a group together yourself (neighbors, friends, organizations). If you arrange a group outing, most places offer discounts.

❑   For the latest **updates** corresponding to the pages in this book, visit our website: **www.KidsLoveTravel.com.**

❑   Each chapter represents an area of the state. Each listing is further identified by city, zip code, and place/event name. Our popular **Activity Index** in the back of the book **lists places by Activity Heading** (i.e. State History, Tours, Outdoors, Museums, etc.).

MISSION STATEMENT

At first glance, you may think that this is a book that just lists hundreds of places to travel. While it is true that we've invested thousands of hours of exhaustive research (*and drove over 3000 miles in Indiana*) to prepare this travel resource...just listing places to travel is not the mission statement of these projects.

As children, Michele and I were able to travel extensively throughout the United States. We consider these family times some of the greatest memories we cherish today. We, quite frankly, felt that most children had this opportunity to travel with their family as we did. However, as we became adults and started our own family, we found that this wasn't necessarily the case. We continually heard friends express several concerns when deciding how to spend "quality" and "quantity" family time. 1) What to do? 2) Where to do it? 3) How much will it cost? 4) How do I know that my kids will enjoy it?

Interestingly enough, as we compare our experiences with our families when we were kids, many of our fondest memories were not made at an expensive attraction, but rather when it was least expected.

It is our belief and mission statement that if you as a family will study and use the contained information to create family memories, these memories will grow a stronger, tighter family. Our ultimate mission statement is, that your children will develop a love and a passion for quality family experiences that they can pass to another generation of family travelers.

We thank you for purchasing this book, and we hope to see you on the road (*and hearing your travel stories!*) God bless your journeys and happy exploring!

George, Michele, Jenny and Daniel

GENERAL INFORMATION

ATHLETICS

- ❑ C – Bloomington. Indiana University Athletics. (866) IUSPORTS or **www.iuhoosiers.com**.
- ❑ C – Indianapolis Tennis Center. IUPUI Campus. (317) 278-2100. RCA Championships. US Tennis Association training site.
- ❑ C – Indianapolis. The Natatorium. Indiana University, 901 West New York Street. (317) 274-3517. Three indoor pools of national and international aquatic events.
- ❑ CE – Lafayette. Purdue University Athletics. (765) 494-3197 or (800) 575-0285 or **www.purduesports.com**
- ❑ CE – Muncie, Ball State University. (765) 285-1474. Mid-American Conference Division I-A. **www.ballstatesports.com**
- ❑ NC – University of Notre Dame. (574) 631-3000 or **http://ndu.fansonly.com** or **http://und.collegesports.com**

BICYCLING

- ❑ Indiana Bicycle Coalition. (800) BIKE-110
- ❑ Hoosier Bikeway System. Department of Natural Resources. (317) 232-4070.

CAMPING

- ❑ Hoosier Camper Guide. (800) 837-7842 or **www.campindiana.org**

CANOEING

- ❑ Get Out & Go Guide. Tourism Division. (317) 232-4070.
- ❑ Liveries listings. **www.indianaoutfitters.com**

COUNTY PARKS & RECREATION DEPARTMENTS

- ❑ C - Hamilton County Department Of Parks & Recreation (317) 896-3811.
- ❑ C - Indianapolis Parks & Recreation (317) 327-PARK. **www.indygov.org/egov/city/dpr/home.htm**
- ❑ C - Monroe County Parks & Recreation (812) 349-2800.
- ❑ CE - Muncie/Delaware County Parks. (765) 747-4858.

- ❑ **CE** - Richmond Parks & Recreation (765) 983-7275.
- ❑ **CW** - Tippecanoe County Parks. (765) 463-2306.
- ❑ **NC** - Cass County Parks & Recreation (574) 753-2928.
- ❑ **NC** - Kokomo Parks & Recreation (317) 452-0063.
- ❑ **NC** – Kosciusko County/Warsaw. (574) 372-9554.
- ❑ **NC** – St. Joseph County Parks (South Bend). (574) 277-4828 or **www.sjcparks.org**.
- ❑ **NE** - Adams County Parks. (260) 724-2520
- ❑ **NE** - Fort Wayne Parks Department (260) 427-6000.
- ❑ **NW** - LaPorte County Parks. (219) 326-6808.

FALL COLOR

- ❑ Peak Fall Color Leaf Line. Department of Natural Resources. (317) 232-4002.

FARM MARKETS

- ❑ Indiana Farm Markets. Get Out & Go Guides. Office of Commissioner of Agriculture. (317) 232-8770.

FISH HATCHERY - STATE RUN

- ❑ **Statewide**
- ❑ Telephone Number: (317) 232-4080. Division of Fish and Wildlife. **www.in.gov/dnr/fishwild/fish/**
- ❑ Hours: Monday - Friday, 8:00am-4:00pm
- ❑ Admission: Free
- ❑ Tours: By appointment
- ❑ Miscellaneous: Sites are Driftwood (Area SE), Avoca (Area SW), Cikana (Area C), Fawn River (Area NE), Twin Branch (Area NC), Mix Sawbah (Area NW), and Bass Lake (Area NW).

State run outdoor fish farms produce 200,000 to 1 million fish each year per site. Any of the six farms might raise trout, large mouth bass, blue gill, sunfish, and black crappie for stocking state parks. The caretakers usually start the tour with a slide show...then, it's out to the ponds. You'll be informed about the proper soil and depth of each pond and the vegetation that is most wanted. At the Avoca site, they have more than enough spring water from a cave nearby to supply their thirteen ponds. The best time to visit is harvest time when they drain the pond down to a minimum pool and wade through the water with a sieve to collect fish. In summer and early winter, the rainbow trout are easiest to see as they jump to the surface when you feed them.

HIKING

❑ Get Out & Go Guide. Tourism Division. (317) 232-4070. **www.in.gov/dnr/outdoor/hike**

HORSEBACK RIDING

❑ Get Out & Go Guide. Tourism Division. (317) 232-4070.

HUNTING & FISHING

❑ Division of Fish and Wildlife. (317) 232-4080.

RECREATION

❑ Indiana Recreation Guide. Department of Natural Resources. (800) 622-4931. **www.in.gov/dnr/parklake/recguide**

SNOWMOBILING

❑ Department of Natural Resources (317) 232-4070
❑ Indiana Snowmobile Association Hotline (574) 679-4006 **www.indianasnowmobilers.com**

STATE PARKS / RESERVOIRS

❑ (317) 232-4124 or (800) 622-4931 or **www.in.gov/dnr/parklake**

THE ARTS

❑ Indiana Arts Commission. (317) 232-1268
❑ Indiana Arts Council. (800) 965-Arts
❑ Arts Indiana Inc. (317) 686-2250

TOURISM

❑ Indiana Tourism (800) 289-6646 or **www.enjoyindiana.com**.
❑ C - Indianapolis Tourism (800) 958-INDY. **www.indy.org**.
❑ NE - Fort Wayne/Allen County CVB – Visitors Center, 1021 South Calhoun (800) 767-7752 or **www.visitfortwayne.com**.

Check out these businesses / services in your area for tour ideas:

AIRPORTS

All children love to visit the airport! Why not take a tour and understand all the jobs it takes to run an airport? Tour the terminal, baggage claim, gates and security / currency exchange. Maybe you'll even get to board a plane.

ANIMAL SHELTERS

Great for the would-be pet owner. Not only will you see many cats and dogs available for adoption, but a guide will show you the clinic and explain the needs of a pet. Be prepared to have the children "fall in love" with one of the animals while they are there!

BANKS

Take a "behind the scenes" look at automated teller machines, bank vaults and drive-thru window chutes. You may want to take this tour and then open a savings account for your child.

CITY HALLS

Halls of Fame, City Council Chambers & Meeting Room, Mayor's Office and famous statues.

ELECTRIC COMPANY / POWER PLANTS

Modern science has created many ways to generate electricity today, but what really goes on with the "flip of a switch". Because coal can be dirty, wear old, comfortable clothes. Coal furnaces heat water, which produces steam, that propels turbines, that drives generators, that make electricity.

FIRE STATIONS

Many Open Houses in October, Fire Prevention Month. Take a look into the life of the firefighters servicing your area and try on their gear. See where they hang out, sleep and eat. Hop aboard a real-life fire engine truck and learn fire safety too.

HOSPITALS

Some Children's Hospitals offer pre-surgery and general tours.

NEWSPAPERS

You'll be amazed at all the new technology. See monster printers and robotics. See samples in the layout department and maybe try to put together your own page. After seeing a newspaper made, most companies give you a free copy (dated that day) as your souvenir. National Newspaper Week is in October.

RESTAURANTS

PIZZA HUT & PAPA JOHN'S

❑ Participating locations

Telephone the store manager. Best days are Monday, Tuesday and Wednesday mid-afternoon. Minimum of 10 people. Small charge per person. All children love pizza – especially when they can create their own! As the children tour the kitchen, they learn how to make a pizza, bake it, and then eat it. The admission charge generally includes lots of creatively made pizzas, beverage and coloring book.

KRISPY KREME DONUTS

❑ Participating locations

Get an "inside look" and learn the techniques that make these donuts some of our favorites! Watch the dough being made in "giant" mixers, being formed into donuts and taking a "trip" through the fryer. Seeing them being iced and topped with colorful sprinkles is always a favorite with the kids. Contact your local store manager. They prefer Monday or Tuesday. Free.

SUPERMARKETS

Kids are fascinated to go behind the scenes of the same store where Mom and Dad shop. Usually you will see them grind meat, walk into large freezer rooms, watch cakes and bread bake and receive free samples along the way. Maybe you'll even get to pet a live lobster!

TV / RADIO STATIONS

Studios, newsrooms, Fox kids clubs. Why do weathermen never wear blue clothes on TV? What makes a "DJ's" voice sound so deep and smooth?

WATER TREATMENT PLANTS

A giant science experiment! You can watch seven stages of water treatment. The favorite is usually the wall of bright buttons flashing as workers monitor the different processes.

U.S. MAIN POST OFFICES

Did you know Ben Franklin was the first Postmaster General (over 200 years ago)? Most interesting is the high-speed automated mail processing equipment. Learn how to address envelopes so they will be sent quicker (there are secrets). To make your tour more interesting, have your children write a letter to themselves and address it with colorful markers. Mail it earlier that day and they will stay interested trying to locate their letter in all the high-speed machinery.

Chapter 1
Central Area - (C)

Our Favorites...

* Mathers' Museum - Bloomington
* Mayberry Cafe - Danville
* Connor Prairie - Fishers
* James Whitcomb Riley Old Home - Greenfield
* Indiana Museum - Indianapolis
* Indianapolis Children's Museum - Indianapolis
* Indianapolis Motor Speedway - Indianapolis
* Indianapolis Zoo - Indianapolis

Future Indy Racing Legend!

HISTORICAL MILITARY ARMOR MUSEUM
2330 North Crystal Street

Anderson 46012

- ☐ Phone: (765) 649-TANK
- ☐ Hours: Tuesday, Thursday, Saturday 1:00-4:00pm
- ☐ Admission: General $3.00 (age 6+). Guided tours $4.50.
- ☐ Tours: Group Tours (for 10 or more) by appointment.

Walk among fully operational and light armor vehicles dating from World War II to Desert Storm. Note President Harry S. Truman's 1947 official Cadillac limousine or the Howe Fire Truck. The building is labeled the "Mess Hall".

ANDERSON FINE ARTS CENTER
32 West 10th Street

Anderson 46015

- ☐ Phone: (765) 649-1248, **Web:** www.andersonart.org
- ☐ Hours: Tuesday-Saturday Noon-5:00pm, Sundays 1:00-5:00pm. Open at 10:00am on Saturdays.
- ☐ Admission: Small. Admission is FREE on Tuesdays and first Sundays.
- ☐ Tours: FRESH tour is $2.00 per person.

The lower level houses a children's hands-on gallery, display areas for temporary exhibitions of student and community art, and a classroom. The FRESH! Tour is of the Arts Center's permanent hands-on gallery for children ages four to twelve. Learn about color, texture, line and form while creating artworks and reproducing famous paintings such as the Mona Lisa and Arrangement in Gray and Black (ex. Whistler's Mother). Included in the ten activity stations are color mixing, spin art, sculptural puzzles, texture rubbings, and a silhouette booth.

ANDERSON SPEEDWAY
1311 Pendleton Avenue

Anderson 46016

❑ Phone: (765) 642-0206

Web: www.andersonspeedway.com

❑ Hours: Fridays Race at 7:30pm (May-August), Saturdays Race at 8:00pm (April-October).

Historic Anderson Speedway is home to weekly racing along with the annual Pay Less/Delco Remy America Little 500 Sprint Car Race and the Pay Less 400-Kendall Late Models. Admission.

ANDERSON SYMPHONY
Paramount Theatre, 1124 Meridian Street

Anderson 46016

❑ Phone: (765) 644-2111 or (888) 644-9490

Web: www.andersonsymphony.org

❑ Admission: $20.00-$25.00 adult, $10.00-$25.00 child.

The recognized Anderson Symphony Orchestra, surrounded by the majestic Moorish architecture, intimate atmosphere and fine acoustics of the circa 1929 theatre make this a grand way to conduct an evening. For kids are concerts with Halloween and Christmas themes and the Youth Orchestra. The Historic theatre has playings of the old theatre organ occasionally, too.

MOUNDS STATE PARK
4306 Mounds Road (I-69 to CR 320 to CR 232)

Anderson 46017

❑ Phone: (765) 642-6627 **Web: www.state.in.us/dnr/parklake/parks/mounds.html**

❑ Admission: $4.00-$5.00 per vehicle.

The park features 10 distinct "earthworks" built by a group of prehistoric Indians known as the Adena-Hopewell people. The largest earthwork, the "Great Mound", is believed to have been constructed around 160 BC. It's a circular enclosure almost ¼ mile in circumference. Stand in the middle and catch the feeling of Ancient tribal ceremonies that might have been held. The nature center is located in the Bronnenberg House (open April-October), which is one of the oldest buildings in the county and was built from materials in the surrounding woods. Bridle Trails, Swimming / Pool.

GIANT EARTH HOME

2928 West Larry Street (Meet at Faulk Park for tours)

Anderson (Pendleton) 46064

- ❑   Phone: (765) 778-2757 **Web: www.giantearthship.com**
- ❑   Hours: Reservations only (May to mid-October)
- ❑   Admission: $6.00 adult, $4.00 student.
- ❑   Tours: Ages 5+, tours begin with 1/2 mile nature hike.

A do-it-yourself home in the woods built by local, Vic Cook. It's powered by solar energy and full of environmental science equipment. The home is made with available materials of stone and scavenged wood. Its rustic design blends well with the patch of woodland that surrounds it, despite the fact that the house is 254 feet long and soars 38 feet high at its tallest point. The kids' most intriguing part is the refrigerator built out of a hollowed birch log using high tech science to keep it cool.

MONROE LAKE STATE RESERVOIR
4850 South SR 446
Bloomington 47401

❑ Phone: (812) 837-9546
www.in.gov/dnr/parklake/reservoirs/monroe.html
❑ Admission: $4.00-$5.00 per vehicle.

Scenic bluffs, rolling hills and lushly wooded areas surround Monroe Lake. Also features a Nature Center and Volleyball Courts, Boating, Camping, Fishing / Ice Fishing, Fourwinds Resort and Marina, Hiking Trails, Boat Rentals, and Swimming / 2 Beaches.

WONDERLAB
308 West Fourth Street (3 blocks west of the bus depot)
Bloomington 47404

❑ Phone: (812) 337-1337, Web: www.wonderlab.org
❑ Hours: Tuesday-Saturday 9:30am-5:00pm, Sunday 1:00-5:00pm. Closed Thanksgiving, Christmas and New Years. Group tours available weekdays 9:00am-2:00pm by reservation.
❑ Admission: $5.50-$6.50 (age 1+).

The Lab provides kid-friendly science experiments like Bubble-Airium, How Things Work, Cosmic Dance, Grapevine climbing, Discovery Garden, and Natural Science (fossils). Each month WonderLab focuses on a different area of science, health and technology. Hands-on activities associated with the program theme change throughout the month. Check the calendar for special guest scientist programs.

INDIANA UNIVERSITY

530 East Kirkwood Avenue, Suite 104 (Indiana Visitor Information Center)

Bloomington 47408

❏ Phone: (812) 856-GOIU, **Web: www.indiana.edu/~iuvis/**
❏ Miscellaneous: Stop by the Indiana Memorial Union (largest student union in the country) for a snack or shop in the bookstore. See separate listing for Mathers Museum located on campus.

Some attractions include:

❏ MEMORIAL STADIUM / ATHLETIC COMPLEX (1001 East 17th Street, 800-447-4648 or 812-855-9618 Stadium). The building houses the IU Department of Intercollegiate Athletics and is the home of the "Hoosiers". Of special interest are the trophy cases in the lobbies, the Athletic Hall of Fame, and the Olympic and NCAA , which hang in the arena. The public is welcome to tour the facilities between the hours of 8:00am-5:00pm, Monday-Friday. Please check-in with the receptionist at the football office complex under the east stands.

❏ LABORATORY OF ARCHAEOLOGY (423 North Fess Street at Ninth Street, 812-855-9544) . A major study and research facility in the field of Hoosier Archaeology. Included in the lab is a public museum devoted to Great Lakes/Ohio Valley archaeology and ethno-history. Hours: Tuesday-Friday 9:00am-4:30pm, Weekends, see exhibit through Mathers Museum. Free.

❏ HILLTOP GARDEN AND NATURE CENTER (2301 East Tenth Street, 812-855-2799). Access is the entrance drive to Tulip Tree Apartments off 10th Street. Home to one of America's oldest youth gardening programs, established in 1948. Greenhouses, ponds and perennials. Call for hours.

Indiana University *(cont.)*

❑   <u>ART MUSEUM/LILLY LIBRARY</u> (Fine Arts Plaza, East Seventh Street, 812-855-5445). Ranked among the nation's best university art museums, the IU Art Museum holds more than 35,000 objects including paintings by such artists as Picasso and Monet. Artworks of the Western World from Byzantine to modern times, Asian and Ancient art, the art of Africa and the Pacific and the Pre-Columbian Americas are all at the museum. The building was designed by the world-renowned architectural firm, I.M. Pei and Partners. Hours: Tuesday-Saturday 10:00am-5:00pm, Sunday Noon-5:00pm. Free.

❑   <u>GREENHOUSE</u> (East Third Street, 812-855-7717). Located next to the I.U. Biology Department building, the Jordan Hall Greenhouse lets you stroll through green gardens, flowers and tropical jungles. It is a thriving greenhouse of unusual, exotic plants from every corner of the world. Individuals may tour during regular business hours. Group tours are available by appointment. Hours: Monday-Friday 8:00am-4:00pm, Saturday & Sunday 9:00am-3:00pm. Free.

❑   <u>KIRKWOOD OBSERVATORY</u> (Dunn Woods -East of Indiana Avenue, near Fourth Street). Built in 1900, the facility contains a 12-inch refractor telescope and other astronomical equipment. Viewing is available every clear Wednesday night when classes are in session.

MATHERS' MUSEUM OF WORLD CULTURES

416 North Indiana Avenue (Northwest side of Indiana University)
University Campus), **Bloomington** 47408

❑ Phone: (812) 855-MUSE
   Web: www.indiana.edu/~mathers/home.html
❑ Hours: Tuesday-Friday 9:00am-4:30pm, Saturday-Sunday
   1:00-4:30pm. Closed during semester breaks.
❑ Admission: FREE. Metered and IU Permit parking is
   available at the McCalla School parking lot on the corner
   of Ninth Street and Indiana Avenue. Parking is available
   on surrounding streets during the weekend.
❑ Tours: Recommended. Guides bring the interactive
   displays to life. Call to schedule.
❑ Miscellaneous: Gift shop with items as low as $0.50. We'd
   recommend that each child purchase a different, unusual
   musical instrument to form a cultural band when they get
   home.

Want to take a trip around the world? This Museum has
exhibits, events, and educational programs that give you a
chance to learn more about objects from Australia to
Zimbabwe... 20,000 artifacts from across the world reveal
traditions, values and beliefs in objects people create and use
every day. The kids hands-on area has pretend houses in a
European Village where you can dress up and play house
from different cultures. Check out "Dancing the Ancestors:
Carnival in South America" and "World Music: Themes and
Variations". After learning about, and sampling their huge
ethnic instrument collection (our favorite part), ask the guide
for assistance in making one of your own using recycled
everyday materials. Unusual and exciting exhibits engage
children here!

MONROE COUNTY HISTORICAL MUSEUM

202 East Sixth Street (6th and Washington Sts.)

Bloomington 47408

❑   Phone: (812) 332-2517

Web: www.kiva.net/~mchm/museum.htm

❑   Hours: Tuesday-Saturday 10:00am-4:00pm, Sundays 1:00-4:00pm.

❑   Admission: FREE, donations requested.

In the old, historic Carnegie Library is the county museum. The giant limestone pot gives you a visible landmark from the Washington Street entrance. "See Stories, Touch Time, Make Memories ! " is their motto. The Permanent Exhibits focus on the worker, education, entertainment, pioneers, and transportation in Monroe County. Many exhibits are set up as walk-up "rooms" of history with genuine artifacts from that era.

BLOOMINGTON SPEEDWAY

5185 South Fairfax Road (3 miles south of town to Old SR 37 South, east at stop light on Fairfax Rd)

Bloomington 47426

❑   Phone: (812) 824-7400

Web: www.bloomingtonspeedway.com

❑   Hours: Generally every Friday (mid-April-September). Pit Gate open at 4:30pm, Grandstand open at 5:30pm, Hot Laps 6:30pm, RACING 7:30pm.

❑   Admission: Average $10.00-$15.00, but may be more for special events. Children 12 and under are FREE.

The fastest quarter mile dirt oval track for sprint, open-wheel modified and street stocks.

CARMEL SYMPHONY ORCHESTRA

PO Box 761

Carmel 46032

❑ Phone: (317) 844-9717.

Web: www.carmelsymphony.org

❑ Season: (September-May). Some outdoor performances during the summer.

❑ Admission: Average $10.00-$15.00.

Family concerts. Enjoy quality musical performances by talented local artists.

MUSEUM OF MINIATURE HOUSES

111 East Main Street (I-465 to Keystone, exit North, one block east of Rangeline), [US 431] to Main Street)

Carmel 46032

❑ Phone: (317) 575-9466

Web: www.museumofminiatures.org

❑ Hours: Wednesday-Saturday 11:00am-4:00pm, Sunday 1:00-4:00pm. Closed in early January and some holidays.

❑ Admission: $4.00 adult, $2.00 child (under 10).

❑ Miscellaneous: Gift Shop

"A world of small things awaits you". See antique and contemporary dollhouses, room boxes, and seasonal displays. Examples: the 1861 dollhouse, a large replica of a person's home; a 1/12th-scale museum within the museum; a house all ready for the daughter's wedding and reception; and collections of unique mini accessories. Children can play the treasure-hunt game.

BARTHOLOMEW COUNTY HISTORICAL SOCIETY MUSEUM

524 Third Street, **Columbus** 47201

❑   Phone: (812) 372-3541
    Web: www.barthist.com/barthist.html
❑   Hours: Tuesday-Friday 9:00am-4:00pm and by
    appointment.
❑   Admission: $4.00 adult, $3.00 senior, $1.00 child (5-17).

The museum is housed in the McEwen-Samuels-Marr home built in 1864. Permanent exhibits include a period bedroom and parlor and a pioneer exhibit from the early 1800's. "The Train Goes Through Town - Columbus, 1886," is an HO Scale Model Train Display of downtown Columbus in the 1886 era. Also featured are hands-on activity areas.

KIDSCOMMONS CHILDREN'S MUSEUM

4th & Washington Streets (The Commons Mall)

Columbus 47201

❑   Phone: (812) 378-3046, **Web: www.kidscommons.org**
❑   Hours: Thursday and Saturday 10:00am-5:00pm, Friday
    10:00am-7:00pm, Sunday 1:00-5:00pm
❑   Admission: $2.00 general (age 2+). Children must be
    accompanied by caregiver.
❑   Miscellaneous: Large indoor children's playground in the
    mall.

The programs here are especially for children 2 to 12 emphasizing science, the visual arts, and community happenings. Activities vary monthly and might include an art-making station where kids may paint, create sculptures or self-portraits, or make inventions with "scrap" material from local industries. Toddlers may gravitate to the tunnels, building blocks and soap bubble station where kids can see how big a bubble they can create and explore why they burst.

For updates, visit our website: www.KidsLoveTravel.com

ZAHARAKO'S CONFECTIONARY

329 Washington Street (off I-65, downtown, across the street from
Commons Mall)

Columbus 47201

❑ Phone: (812) 379-9329

Web: www.kid-at-art.com/htdoc/zaharako.html

❑ Hours: Monday-Thursday 10:00am-4:00pm, Friday-
Saturday 10:00am-5:00pm.

A Columbus landmark and a "must-see" for kids is located downtown. Popular from the day it opened on October 20, 1900, The Greeks, or Zaharako's Confectionery as it is known today, was founded by three brothers from Greece. At the time, it was common for settlers from abroad to become shopkeepers. "Zaharaoplastion" is Greek for Confectionery. Zaharako's is known for its turn-of-the-century decor; a self-playing, German pipe organ installed in 1908; two onyx soda fountains (once on display at the St. Louis World's Fair) installed in 1905; Christmas decorations; and the Cheese-Br-ger, Hot Fudge Sundae, and other menu items. Fun names like "Fireball", "Double Up" or "Double Down" are called out with many orders.

HENDRICKS COUNTY HISTORICAL MUSEUM

170 South Washington, **Danville** 46122

❑ Phone: (765) 745-9617

❑ Hours: Thursday 10:00am-4:00pm and Saturday 1:00-4:00pm.

❑ Admission: Donations accepted.

Located in the former sheriff's residence and jail (1866-1974). Visit and have your picture taken in "jailbird" attire. Also, see items relating to domestic life, agriculture, military history and education.

CONNER PRAIRIE

13400 Allisonville Road (NE of Indianapolis, I-465, exit 35 or I-69, exit 5)

Fishers 46038

❑ Phone: (317) 776-6006 or (800) 966-1836
   Web: www.connerprairie.org
❑ Hours: Tuesday-Saturday 9:30am-5:00pm (closed Tuesdays in April & November), Sunday 11:00am-5:00pm (April-November). Closed Mondays, Easter, Thanksgiving, Christmas Eve & Day and New Years Eve and Day. EST
❑ Admission: $11.00 adult, $10.00 senior (65+), $7.00 child (5-12) (April-November). Half Price (December).
❑ Miscellaneous: 1823 William Conner House is a restored settler's and statesman's home - the finest in town. Tours every 20 minutes for $1.50 additional charge. Museum Center exhibits, gift shop and Persimmons Restaurant (lunch/dinner). Programs range from the joyful festivity of an 1836 wedding to the dark uncertainty of the Underground Railroad.

Unlike many other historical villages in the Midwest, when you enter Prairietown, you really do interact as if you've been transported in time! All of the townspeople dress and act their character according to the year 1836. Mention of modern conveniences like pagers and cell phones is responded to with a blank stare. Your initial conversations may be a little awkward but you get the feel of things quickly. Pretend you're staying the night at the Golden Eagle Inn (for 12 ½ cents!) and then walk through town to visit neighbors like the Quaker printer, Jeremiah Hudson, or the Fentons (weavers - you can purchase yarn dyed naturally), or the Campbells (Dr. and Mrs. - definitely upper class). The kids' favorites were the baby lambs just born in the Conner

Barn and the Schoolhouse. Sit on split log benches as the school master gives you lessons teaching the "loud" school method. Youngsters recite their different lessons aloud. Repetition is the key to learning and a ruler is used to discipline (not used on your first day of school, of course). Allow enough time to spend with chores like candle dipping, washing clothes on a washboard, spinning, gardening or by playing with 19th century toys in the yard.

JAMES WHITCOMB RILEY OLD HOME AND MUSEUM

250 West Main Street (I-70 to SR 9 to US 40, East of Indianapolis)

Greenfield 46140

❑   Phone: (317) 462-8539

   Web: www.greenfieldin.org/parks/riley_museum.asp

❑   Hours: Monday-Saturday 10:00am-4:00pm (April to early November).

❑   Admission: $3.00 adult, $1.00 child (6-17).

❑   Tours: Every half hour.

Mr. Riley was born in Greenfield in 1849 and his 1044 poems brought him the name, Hoosier Poet. (They are mostly about Indiana and kids). Famous characters he developed were the Raggedy Man, Little Orphan Annie and Old Aunt Mary from people he talked with and observed, or, events like the circus in town or a harvest festival. The best parts of the tour are the winding, creaky staircase, the rafter room, a cubby-hole and the chimney flue. Each spot plays a part in one of Riley's ghost stories. Little Orphan Annie used to tell stories that always ended "Er the Gobble-uns'll get you-ef you don't watch out!". Our guide recited several of these adapted, story poems with us throughout the tour - it was a delightful way to add mystique to a very simple home.

PRESIDENT BENJAMIN HARRISON HOME

1230 North Delaware Street (just north off I-65)

Indianapolis 46202

❑ Phone: (317) 631-1888
  Web: www.presidentbenjaminharrison.org
❑ Hours: Monday-Saturday 10:00am-3:30pm. Sundays in July, August & September only 12:30-3:30pm. The museum is closed all major holidays, 500 Race Day, and the first three weeks in January.
❑ Admission: $6.00 adult, $5.00 senior, $3.00 student.
❑ Tours: Begin every 30 minutes, approximately 1 hour
❑ Miscellaneous: Gift Shop

See the 16 room Italianate Victorian home of the lawyer nominated for 23rd presidency in 1888. Harrison actually campaigned from his front porch here and his daughter loved to sneak and slide down the three-story spiral staircase. Stand on the front stoop where Benjamin Harrison gave 80 "front porch" speeches to 300,000 people who came by to listen. In the master bedroom is displayed an old-fashioned home gym with weighted pulleys made from beautiful wood (a 19th century NordicTrack!) See the Library where election returns were tallied by telegraph. View a piece of Haviland White House china that Caroline Harrison designed choosing corn to surround the border because it was "a crop indigenous to the North American Continent". See creations of the First Lady, Caroline's paintings. Actual belongings of the Harrisons include an inaugural Bible, White House Tea Set and Parlor Sofa – but don't touch! Look for several unusual, specially designed, chairs Harrison loved. Your kids will really feel that one day, even they, could be a President after visiting here! Nice job.

ATOMIC BOWL / ACTION BOWL

1105 Prospect (I-70 exit 83A or I-65 exit 111/Fletcher, turn right, turn left on Virginia Ave)

Indianapolis 46203

❑ Phone: (317) 686-6006
   Web: www.fountainsquareindy.com
❑ Hours: Monday-Thursday 11:00am-9:00pm, Friday-Saturday 11:00am-Midnight-ish, Sunday Noon-5:00pm.
❑ Admission: $18.00 per hour per lane (up to 6 can bowl one lane). $2.50 shoe rental per pair.

The Fountain Diner is the biggest diner we've ever visited – bring the whole gang along. Definitely try their shakes, floats and a grilled chili dog. Two Duckpin Bowling Alleys each represent a different period of time. Action Bowl is on the 4th floor and has been restored to the original time period of the building: the 1930's. Atomic Bowl is on the basement level and has been restored to the 1950's era. The Atomic features two juke boxes that play 45's with songs from the period. There's also a Soda Fountain serving hand-dipped shakes, malts, root beer floats, and ice cream sodas. Duckpin bowling is very kid-friendly. The balls are just a little larger than softballs and are easily handled, even by toddlers. The duckpin bowling is so fun and silly, skill isn't really an issue (at least, not for us!)

BALLET INTERNATIONALE

502 N. Capitol Avenue, Suite B (performances at Murat Centre)

Indianapolis 46204

❑ Phone: (317) 637-8979 or Box Office (317) 921-6444.
   Web: www.balletinternationale.org
❑ Season: (September-April). Performances evenings at 7:00 or 8:00pm, matinees at 2:00pm.

Ballet Internationale *(cont.)*

❑   Admission: $20.00-$50.00 adult, $20.00-$30.00 students
(13-18), $10.00-$40.00 child (3-12).

Ballet Internationale is an ensemble offering a variety of
full-length fairy tale ballets, contemporary repertoire and an
annual production of The Nutcracker.

EITELJORG MUSEUM OF AMERICAN INDIAN AND WESTERN ART

500 West Washington Street (White River State Park)

Indianapolis 46204

❑   Phone: (317) 636-9378, **Web: www.eiteljorg.org**
❑   Hours: Tuesday-Saturday 10:00am-5:00pm, Sunday Noon-
5:00pm. Open Mondays, Memorial Day through Labor
Day. Closed Thanksgiving, Christmas Eve, Christmas and
New Year's Day.
❑   Admission: $7.00 adult, $6.00 senior (65+), $4.00 child (5-
17) and full-time students w/ID.
❑   Tours: Daily 1:00 pm.
❑   Miscellaneous: Award-winning store offers authentic art,
clothing, home décor. Many festivals held throughout the
year.

The Eiteljorg Museum is unique, one of two museums east
of the Mississippi with both Native American and Western
art. Contemporary artists who tell the story of today's West
are represented and the Native American collection includes
pottery, basketry, sculpture and other artifacts from all 10
North American native cultural areas. Kid's Indian crafts or
demonstrations offered. Pick up the Family Guide listing of
activities and questions to answer. You'll feel you walked
into a Santa Fe courtyard as you tour the rooms.

INDIANA STATE MUSEUM

White River State Park Museum Complex (between Hall of
Champions and Eiteljorg Museum)

Indianapolis 46204

❑   Phone: (317) 232-1637, **Web: www.in.gov/ism/**
❑   Hours: Monday-Saturday 9:00am-4:45pm, Sunday Noon-
4:45pm.
❑   Admission: $7.00 adult, $6.50 senior, $4.00 child (3-12).
❑   Miscellaneous: Gift shop with many Indiana-made items.

Pick up a child's passport and press one stamp at each
station along the tour route (this really keeps the kids
interested). The "Make the Call" exhibit is where you try to
simulate various bird/animal calls – then play them back to
see how you did. Ever seen a batfish? Beware of the Wholly!
Many "touch me", "listen to me" and especially "smell"
stations(!) add to the living history. A café is upstairs to
catch a snack or lunch. Come back later, or fit in, an IMAX
six-story movie located in the lobby (for an extra fee).

INDIANA PACERS

125 Pennsylvania Street (Conseco Fieldhouse)

Indianapolis 46204

❑   Phone: (317) 917-2100, **Web: www.nba.com/pacers/**

NBA Basketball. Boomer, the Panther OR Bowser, the Dog
are the fun team mascots and there's a fan club and kids
pages/games on the website.

INDIANA SOLDIERS' AND SAILORS' MONUMENT/ COLONEL ELI LILLY CIVIL WAR MUSEUM

(Monument Circle - Meridian Street, Center of Town...You can't miss it!)

Indianapolis 46204

❑ Phone: (317) 232-7615
   Web: www.state.in.us/iwm/civilwar/index.html
❑ Hours: Daily 11:00am-7:00pm. Access to Museum and Deck is more limited, call first if making special trip.
❑ Admission: FREE
❑ Tours: Observation deck open mid-April to mid-October.
❑ Miscellaneous: The USS Indianapolis Memorial, five blocks west, is of historical significance also.

Challenge your energetic kids to the 336 stair climb to the glass-enclosed balcony at the top for a panoramic view. (An elevator is available up to the last 45 stairs). See many bronze and limestone carvings (enormous and detailed) of famous Indianans like James Riley and President Harrison. The largest sculptures are of Civil Wartime Scenes. Throughout the year, the monument's steps play to performers, politicians and festivals. Inside the base is a museum with interesting city and war insights telling the personal stories of Hoosiers who fought to protect the Union and supported the Civil War effort. "Miss Indiana" tops the landmark with curved steps North and South and fountains with reflecting pools to the East and West.

INDIANA STATE CAPITOL BUILDING

200 West Washington Street (corner of Capitol Ave. and
Washington St)

Indianapolis 46204

❑ Phone: (317) 232-9410 (when General Assembly is in
session) . (317) 233-5293 (rest of year)
Web: www.in.gov/statehouse/tour

❑ Hours: Monday-Friday 8:30am-4:30pm, excluding
holidays.

❑ Admission: FREE

❑ Tours: Tours of the State House every weekday, excluding
holidays. Weekend tours are offered Saturday and Sunday
at 10:15am, 11:00am, 12:00pm and 1:00pm. You must
enter at the North door. Self-guided tour booklets are
always available at the Information Desk. Self-guided tour
booklets are always available at the Information Desk or in
Room 220.

Built in 1882 (on the site of the 1835 State House) with
Indiana limestone, the building contains executive,
legislative, and judicial offices. There's a Rotunda in the
middle with North, South, East, and West wings. See the
Governor's office with the state-seal rug. Even some door
knobs are embossed with the state seal - nice touch. Also, his
desk is made from teak decking from the USS Indiana. Sit in
on the General Assembly State Supreme Court when in
session (older, quiet kids only) beginning in January.
Supreme Court matters tend to be dealing with serious,
thought-provoking issues. Stories of things found during the
last major renovation are engaging. The glass domes above
are beautiful to look up at.

INDIANAPOLIS HORSE-DRAWN CARRIAGE RIDES

(Downtown)

Indianapolis 46204

❑ Admission: Average $30.00-$35.00 per ride for up to 4 people (30 minute ride).

❑ Tours: Reservations accepted. Usually parked in front of major downtown hotels and Circle Centre Mall.

Circle City Carriages (317) 387-1516

Blue Ribbon Carriage Co. (317) 631-4169

Yellow Rose Carriage (317) 634-3400

INDIANAPOLIS SYMPHONY ORCHESTRA

45 Monument Circle (Hibert Circle Theatre)

Indianapolis 46204

❑ Phone: (317) 639-4300 or (800) 366-8457
   Web: www.indyorch.org

❑ Admission: $10.00-30.00 adult, $6.00-17.00 child (4-12).

Yuletide Celebration concerts, Family series, and Symphony on the Prairie Summer outdoor concerts.

MADAME C. J. WALKER THEATRE CENTER

617 Indiana Avenue (A few blocks from White River Park)

Indianapolis 46204

❑ Phone: (317) 236-2099
   Web: www.madamecjwalker.com

❑ Hours: Monday, Wednesday, Thursday, Friday 9:00am-5:00pm, Tuesday 11:00am-5:00pm.

❑ Admission: FREE. Special events require a fee.

❑ Tours: By appointment. 30 minutes

❏ Miscellaneous: Asante Theatre programs for children (ages 8-18 years) to perform original plays centered on African American culture and current issues. Admission.

Because Madame Walker worked long hours and ate poorly, she began losing her hair. Frustrated, she cooked up different ingredients in her kitchen trying to find a solution that would make hair grow full and healthy. When she found a combination, neighbors began asking for some. Soon, she was advertising in newspapers and filling orders by mail. Madame created a line of shampoo, hair grower and oil treatments and began the first cosmetic direct sales. Known as the nation's first woman millionaire, the Center is a restoration of the former 1920's headquarters of her cosmetic business. Now it is a cultural showcase for the city's African American community. The theatre is decorated with African motif from collections of journeys to Africa. There is a small museum section in the Center that highlights artifacts from the entrepreneur's life and business.

PEEWINKLE'S PUPPET STUDIO

25 East Henry Street, downtown (five blocks south of the Circle Centre)

Indianapolis 46204

❏ Phone: (317) 283-7144 or (800) 849-4853
   www.nashville-indiana.com/Attractions/puppet/show.html
❏ Admission: $5.00-$10.00 fee (free popcorn)

This old-world style intimate puppet theatre is complete with puppet gallery, 12' x 17' stage, full lighting, lobby and workshop capabilities. Puppets are available for sale. MMHP Puppet Productions present performances, field trips, workshops, birthdays and private events.

WHITE RIVER STATE PARK
801 West Washington Street (Downtown)

Indianapolis 46204

❑   Phone: (800) 665-9056 or (317) 233-2434
   Web: www.in.gov/dnr/parklake/parks/whiteriver.html
❑   Miscellaneous: Pedal boat and bicycle rentals.

Here's a state park for those not in the mood to camp, hike, swim, fish or hunt bugs. You'll find trails, grassy areas, and waterways at White River State Park, just like you'd expect to see in any other state park. That, however is where the similarities end. White River State Park has cultural, educational and recreational attractions, too. A half mile Riverwalk Promenade made of Indiana limestone offers beautiful waterways, lots of grassy areas and tree-lined boulevards. The Pumphouse Visitors Center, IMAX 3D Theater, Eiteljorg Museum, The Indianapolis Zoo, NCAA Hall of Champions, Indiana Museum, Victory Field and The National Institute for Fitness and Sport are all within the park boundaries and offer some of the best cultural entertainment in the state.

NCAA HALL OF CHAMPIONS
700 West Washington Street (One NCAA Plaza)

Indianapolis 46206

❑   Phone: (317) 917-6222 or (800) 735-6222
   Web: www.ncaa.org/hall_of_champions/global/home.htm
❑   Hours: Tuesday-Saturday 10:00am-5:00pm, Sunday Noon-5:00pm. Open Mondays in the summer.
❑   Admission: $3.00 adult, $2.00 student (age 6+).
❑   Miscellaneous: Souvenir gift shop complete with exclusive NCAA merchandise.

The two-level Hall of Champions features four presentation theaters, a 144-monitor video wall, numerous interactive and hands-on displays, a turn-of-the-century gymnasium and a unique view of the sports world via the "Look Up to Champions" video display. From the "who, what and where" basics to our most recent headlines, this is where they celebrate March Madness year-round. The presentations in the Coaches' Locker Room and the Student-Athletes' Classroom provide an insightful glimpse into the world of college athletics. Listen to your team's fight song or find out what it takes to make a champion. Shoot hoops on an old-fashioned half court. Do you have what it takes?

INDIANAPOLIS CHILDREN'S CHOIR

4600 Sunset Avenue (Butler University)

Indianapolis 46208

❏   Phone: (317) 940-9640

Having grown to a program of over 1,200 singers in 12 choirs, the Indianapolis Children's Choir continues to be one of the largest and most accomplished children's choral programs in the nation. In residence on the campus of Butler University, the choir makeup reflects the diversity of central Indiana (singers come from 17 counties). In addition to its own concert series, the choir performs regularly with professional symphony orchestras including the Indianapolis Symphony Orchestra and has also performed with The Chieftains and Celine Dion. The Indianapolis Children's Choir has also performed several times at Carnegie Hall and regularly tours both nationally and internationally.

INDIANAPOLIS CHILDREN'S MUSEUM

3000 North Meridian Street (30th Street between Meridian and
Illinois Streets - SR 37 North)

Indianapolis 46208

❑ Phone: (317) 334-3322

Web: www.childrensmuseum.org

❑ Hours: Monday-Sunday 10:00am-5:00pm (March-Labor
Day). Closed Mondays rest of year. Closed Easter Day,
Thanksgiving Day and Christmas Day.

❑ Admission: $11.50 adult, $10.50 senior (60+), $6.50 child
(2-17). Free first Thursdays from 5:00-8:00pm.

❑ Miscellaneous: Annual passes available.

Be sure that your kids have a good nap or plan multiple visits, because this place is full of 5 floors of fun! The well-known museum is as good as they say it is – a must visit! The largest and most popular children's museum in the world includes these areas:

❑ THE LARGEST WATER CLOCK IN THE WORLD -
Located at entrance & a marvel to watch-looks like a giant
science fair project.

❑ PASSPORT TO THE WORLD - Cultures and people.
Look through cutouts facing a mirror to see yourself
dressed as a kid from another country or try your hand at
playing foreign instruments or watching a performance.

❑ PLAYSCAPE - Baby area with super soft play/crawl area
and water, sand, garden, dress up, play house, areas for
pre- schoolers.

❑ SPACE QUEST PLANETARIUM - 3 D flight and
simulated star. Projection laser light shows to modern
"hip" music and characters ("Garfield")

❑ EGYPTIAN TOMB - A 2700 year old real mummy with
walk-along displays that teach you materials & scents used
to prepare a body.

For updates, visit our website: www.KidsLoveTravel.com

❑   SCIENCE WORKS - Send the pre-schoolers over to
     Playscape. School-aged children are hands-on with the
     Dock Shop multi-station water learning and construction
     site with stations where kids (using safe, scaled down
     material) pretend and play in all phases of constructing a
     new building.

❑   DINOSPHERE - one of the largest displays of juvenile
     and family dinosaur fossils in the nation. The experience
     features real dinosaur fossils in a realistic, interactive
     setting that encourages families to search for clues about
     why dinos lived and died.

❑   Our favorites are still ALL ABOARD! Sitting in the train
     car taking a short ride on the rails. Speakers and woofers in
     the seats and video screens of moving scenery in the
     windows create the illusion of movement. We also really
     like PUPPETS. You can try shadow, body or
     ventriloquist shows. Can you keep your mouth closed
     when saying "want" (say "oooh-ont)?

INDIANAPOLIS JUNIOR CIVIC THEATRE

1200 West 38th Street

Indianapolis 46208

❑   Phone: (317) 924-6770. Box Office, (317) 923 - 4597
     Web: www.civictheatre.org/youth.html

1st – 8th grade productions each season with its main stage
productions ranging from acclaimed musicals to comedies
and dramas. Productions might include Rumpelstiltskin, as
well as The Velveteen Rabbit, Winnie the Pooh and
Charlotte's Web.

INDIANAPOLIS MUSEUM OF ART

1200 West 38th Street (38th and Michigan)

Indianapolis 46208

❑ Phone: (317) 920-2660, **Web: www.ima-art.org**
❑ Hours: Wednesday-Saturday 10:00am-5:00pm, Sunday Noon-5:00pm. Open late on Thursday. Closed Thanksgiving, Christmas, and New Years.
❑ Admission: FREE
❑ Tours: Daily at 1:00pm. Also, Thursday at 7:00pm.
❑ Miscellaneous: Snack area/café and Garden Terrace restaurant (Open for lunch only).

The Indianapolis Museum of Art is among the largest general art museums in the U.S., with a collection of 42,000 works that spans the range and scope of art history. Known for Oriental art, American prints and glass sculpture, African and Indiana artists. Popular Art Making Classes or Family Days are a series of Sunday afternoon events featuring self-guided tours, studio art-making activities and related performances for families with children ages 5 to 10.

FORT HARRISON STATE PARK

5753 Glenn Road (Off I-465 & 56th Street)

Indianapolis 46216

❑ Phone: (317) 591-0904
Web: www.in.gov/dnr/parklake/parks/ftharrison.html

The Fort - (317) 543-9592. Golf Resort and Harrison House Suites & 3 Officer's Homes, plus dining. Landscape and history are blended in a unique setting at the 1700-acre park featuring walking and jogging trails, picnic sites, fishing access to Fall Creek and two national historic districts. The former Citizen's Military Training Camp, Civilian Conservation Corps camp, and World War II prisoner of war camp is preserved at the park headquarters location. Many plan hikes after visiting the interpretive center exhibits and talking with park naturalists. Others go bird watching for woodpeckers and warblers amongst the wildflowers in the forest. Bridle/biking trails and fishing are here, too.

INDIANA STATE POLICE YOUTH EDUCATION AND HISTORICAL CENTER

8500 East 21st Street (Off 1-70, east of downtown)

Indianapolis 46219

❑   Phone: (317) 899-8293
❑   Hours: Monday-Friday 8:00am-Noon and 1:00-4:00pm
❑   Admission: Donation
❑   Tours: Groups by appointment.

To teach respect for the police force or to pretend to be an officer for awhile – here's the place to go. Police vehicles are everywhere - restored classics, miniature police cars from every state or you can sit in a real car (turn on lights, sirens or intercom radio). Also, see displays and firearms; exhibit of Indiana's own John Dillinger; or bicycle safety.

INDIANAPOLIS MOTOR SPEEDWAY

4790 West 16th Street

Indianapolis 46222

❑   Phone: (317) 484-6784
     Web: www.indy500.com/museum
❑   Hours: Daily 9:00am-5:00pm (except Christmas Day)
❑   Admission: General Admission $1-3.00 track tour, $1-3.00 museum (ages 6 and under free). Grounds tours $10.00-$25.00 per person (see details on next page).
❑   Tours: By mini-bus, weather permitting.
❑   Miscellaneous: Gift shop. Home of the Indy 500 and the NASCAR Brickyard 400.

Indianapolis Motor Speedway *(cont.)*

Drive right onto the inside track as you are awed by the size of the speedway. Built initially as a proving ground for autos, it developed into the largest one day sporting event in the world and the greatest spectacle in racing – the Indy 500. The Hall of Fame Museum contains over 75 vehicles and numerous artifacts and trivia videos. Antique motorized vehicles, race winning cars, pace cars and even a rocket – boosted car can be seen. Stop in the theatre to view a film of race highlights. Maybe the best part of your visit will be the racetrack bus tour. Adrenaline is pumping as you make one lap with a narrative around each turn. There is nothing like the view as you approach the first turn – scary normally, but comforting to know the bus is only going 35 mph! The start/finish line has one strip of the original brick track. The black and white checkered victory circle actually raises the winning car and driver high into the air so all spectators can see. You'll also get a view of Gasoline Alley where drivers and mechanics spend pre-race time pampering their cars. If you've already visited the Hall of Fame Museum and taken the Track Tour, maybe now it's time to try the Speedway Grounds Tours - held one weekend each month (June-September). Each 1 ½ hour tour provides an insider's look at over 90 years of history with tour stops at the Museum, Gasoline Alley Suites, Start/Finish Line, Track Tour, WorldComplex, Pagoda (timing & scoring), Victory Platform and Garage Area. The gift shop has no trouble selling souvenirs to the starry-eyed visitors who can only dream of such speed.

INDIANAPOLIS ZOO/ WHITE RIVER GARDENS

1200 West Washington Street (in White River Park from West Street exits off major interstates)

Indianapolis 46222

❑   Phone: (317) 630-2001, **Web: www.indyzoo.com** and **www.whiterivergardens.com**

❑   Hours: Daily, 9:00am - 4:00pm. (Extended Hours, May-August). Closed Monday and Tuesday (January-February). Gardens have more restricted hours, especially Fall and Winter seasons.

❑   Admission: $8.00-$12.50 adult, senior, youth (age 2-12).

❑   Miscellaneous: Stroller rental. Parking $5.00. Gift shop. Also, check out the train rides, antique carousel, horse-drawn trolley or pony, camel and elephant rides. The adventuresome will like the only Indy coaster, Kombo safari family coaster. The Enchanted Mill playground is the perfect place for kids to burn off some steam and, on hot days, cool off. A section of the playground has water jets that shoot up from the ground, along with a "dolphin" and "seal" that squirt water.

The 64 acre cage-less zoo is home to simulated habitats featuring deserts, plains, forests and the ocean. Get inspired in the Gardens by the most unique and beautiful botanical attraction in the Midwest. Highlights are the Water Garden, Sun & Shade Gardens, and, for kids especially, the Motion Garden and the Mist Garden. *(continued next page)*

Here's some things to look for in the zoo:

❑ WATERS BIOME - consists of the Dolphin Pavilion, the Waters Building housing the Zoo's fish, marine birds, amphibians and the Amazon exhibit, and the walrus, seal, sea lion and polar bear marine mammal exhibits. The only dolphin shows in Indiana are daily (at performance or underwater level).

❑ DESERTS BIOME - The 80-foot diameter transparent dome allows the animals to bask in natural sunlight year-round while heating and air conditioning vents hidden in the rocks keep the temperature in the 80's. Free roaming desert plants and animals co-exist as they would in nature. Giant cacti, lizards, and iguanas roam the dome.

❑ ENCOUNTERS AREA - domestic animal shows and interaction with zookeepers and animals. "EdZootainment" combines education and entertainment.

❑ FORESTS BIOME - include Amur (Siberian) tigers, golden lion tamarins, and red pandas. Lena, one of the Zoo's Amur tigers, was wild-caught in Siberia after poachers shot her mother.

❑ PLAINS BIOME - kudu and zebras grazing in their large yard along with ostriches, vultures and other birds, giraffes pluck leaves from trees, and elephants. East African crowned cranes and Marabou storks rest near a pond or see African lions, African elephants and African wild dogs.

If you get there at opening, you can often watch feeding time. Our favorite area, the Waters Biome, has polars, penguins and puffins. The best part is the Dolphin Show. Sit in the splash area if you want to have a good look up-close and maybe you'll be picked to help the dolphins do tricks! Did you know dolphins have belly buttons? What we liked best about the outdoor exhibits throughout the zoo was the combination of animals in their natural spaces, sharing space with other creatures you would find in the wild. It's like a giant scavenger hunt – seek and find!

INDIANAPOLIS INDIANS BASEBALL

501 West Maryland Street (games at Victory Field)

Indianapolis 46225

❑ Phone: (317) 269-3542, **Web:** www.indyindians.com

The AAA International League Indians play games at Victory Field, April to early September. The Indians are affiliated with the Pittsburgh Pirates and have been Indianapolis' professional baseball team for a while. If you are able to make it to a game, make sure to look for Rowdie. This fuzzy red bear loves to see smiling fans at the ballpark! Rowdie may even give you a high five, sign an autograph or deliver a pizza to your seat!

INDIANAPOLIS RACEWAY PARK

10267 E. US Hwy 136 (three miles west of Clermont in Hendricks County)

Indianapolis 46234

❑ Phone: (317) 293-RACE or (800) 884-6472 tickets

Web: www.irponline.com

❑ Season: March - October.

IRP features three unique tracks, drawing the biggest names in racing from the NHRA to NASCAR and USAC for annual events at the complex (US National Drag Racing, midgets, sprints, USAC Silver Crown and Kroger Speedfest).

INDIANAPOLIS COLTS

7001 West 56th Street (home games in the RCA Dome)

Indianapolis 46254

❑   Phone: (317) 297-7000, **Web: www.colts.com**

NFL Football and the Colts Kids Club package are a little football fan's dream. Two hours before every Colts home game thousands of Colts fans gather on Pam Am Plaza for a huge pre-game party for the family. There are tons of games and prizes to win in the C. P. Morgan Fun Zone. Kidz Klub Corner has Free Popcorn, free Cotton Candy, Free Face Painting and Temporary Tattoos, Remote Control X-Terra Truck Contest, and Slide and Helmet Bouncer Inflatables.

BEEF & BOARDS DINNER THEATRE

9301 North Michigan Road (I-465 & U.S. 421 (Michigan Rd, Exit 27) just behind the Holiday Inn)

Indianapolis 46268

❑   Phone: (317) 876-0519, **Web: www.beefandboards.com**
❑   Admission: The $9.00 admission includes the show and a beverage and small snack.

Beef & Boards Dinner Theatre continues to serve up fun, food and fabulous live entertainment. Try a matinee at the Children's Theatre productions at the BEEF & BOARDS. Kids (ages preschool to 6th grade) and their adults can watch a one hour show either Friday or Saturday mornings or early afternoons.

CARIBBEAN COVE INDOOR WATERPARK

Holiday Inn Select North @ the Pyramids. 3850 DePauw Blvd. (I-465 exit 27, Michigan Road)

Indianapolis 46268

❑ Phone: (317) 872-9790
   Web: www.caribbeancovewaterpark.com

❑ Hours: Daily 9:00am-10:00pm (11:00pm on weekends). Check in time is 4:00pm. Check out time is 11:00am.

❑ Admission: $139.00-$189.00 per night for up to five per room. Waterpark wristbands included.

Jump into a tropical paradise at Caribbean Cove Indoor Water Park where registered hotel guests find fabulous fun. It's an indoor tropical island full of surprises, splashes, squirts, sprays, slides and waterfalls. One of the main attractions is Kastaway Kidz Island featuring a 700-gallon bucket dumping station that soaks guests every 6-8 minutes. The dumping bucket sets high atop a highly interactive shipwrecked boat playscape designed specifically with your little squirts in mind. Now, catch a ride on a raft and drift lazily around in the leisure river. Then, hold on tight for the ride of your life on two 40 foot tall aqua whiz tube slides (part of the ride goes outside!). The not-so-faint-of-heart can climb aboard a super long flume slide sending them spiraling throughout the park. Sports enthusiasts will have a ball in the sports activity pool and the Holidome recreation center or Crazy CoCo's arcade. Refresh and refill in assorted cafes and restaurants - all indoors.

DONALDSON'S FINER CHOCOLATES

600 So. State Road 39 (I-65 north to State Road 39 exit)

Lebanon 46052

❑ Phone: (765) 482-3334

❑ Tours: Group size limited to 20-25 people. Call ahead to arrange.

Now, say you're passing through Lebanon on I-65 and suddenly you can't go one more minute without some fabulous chocolate. No problem. Donaldson's Finer Chocolates is just a stone's throw off the highway and well worth the stop. Or, you can plan ahead and call to set up a tour. Tours cover the history of the company and the making of the chocolate. See the candy makers at work, and taste the "chocolate bark" that's made on marble slabs while you watch. There are dozens of other treats you'll want to try, too.

MORGAN-MONROE STATE FOREST

6220 Forest Road (8 miles east of SR 37)

Martinsville 46151

❑ Phone: (765) 342-4026, **Web: www.in.gov/dnr/forestry**

❑ Miscellaneous: Camping, Hiking trails,

Morgan-Monroe State Forest encompasses more than 24,000 acres in Morgan and Monroe counties in south central Indiana. The forest land encompasses many steep ridges and valleys, and is forested with some of the state's finest hardwoods. The original settlers of the area cleared and attempted to farm the ridges, but were frustrated by rocky soil unsuitable for agriculture. The highlight here might be Draper Cabin (if you can get a reservation). The use of this cabin is a unique experience. No other Indiana state forest offers the opportunity to rent an old log cabin and return to a time 110 years ago when the fireplace provided heat and food was prepared over the burning coals. Three forest lakes, Bryant Creek Lake (9 acres), Cherry Lake (4 acres) and Prather Lake (4 acres) are all open to fishing and boating, but not swimming. Gold Panning is permitted in Morgan-Monroe and Yellowwood State Forests.

ALEXANDER CARRIAGE RIDES
Franklin and VanBuren Streets (Next to Old Bartley House)

Nashville 47448

❑ Phone: (812) 988-8230
❑ Hours: Daily, weather permitting

Horse-drawn carriage rides with Tim, the driver and his horse, Dan. Interesting sites are pointed out throughout downtown.

BROWN COUNTY HISTORICAL MUSEUM
Museum Lane, Downtown, **Nashville 47448**

❑ Phone: (812) 988-6089
❑ Hours: Weekends and Holidays 1:00-5 :00pm. (May-October)
❑ Admission: Donations

An 1897 Doctor's Office, blacksmith, loom room, 1879 log jail (men were kept downstairs, women upstairs) and 1850's pioneer cabin.

BROWN COUNTY STATE PARK
State Road 46 East or West, **Nashville 47448**

❑ Phone: (812) 988-6406.
   Web: www.browncountystatepark.com
❑ Admission: $4.00-$5.00 per vehicle.

Cabins & Abe Martin Lodge. (812) 988-4418. Accommodations and Restaurant. Nearby excursions are at

Yellowwood State Forest (rare trees) or T.C. Steele State Memorial. Indiana's largest state park also has camping, horse camping and riding trails, hiking trails, naturalist services, scenic driving, picnicking, fishing and swimming.

MELCHIOR MARIONETTE THEATRE

South VanBuren Street (west side of street)

Nashville 47448

❑ Phone: (800) 849-4853

 www.nashville-indiana.com/Attractions/puppet/show.html

❑ Shows: 1:00 & 3:00 pm, Saturday & Sunday (July-October)

❑ Admission: $2.50 general (popcorn is free), purchased 15 minutes before Showtime at the theatre. Call for schedule.

Second and third generations of Melchiors specialize in performing with beautiful hand-crafted and costumed marionettes. The charming sixty seat outdoor theatre in downtown Nashville is where the half-life size handcrafted marionettes perform 20 minute Cabaret shows.

NASHVILLE EXPRESS TRAIN TOURS

Franklin and Van Buren Streets

Nashville 47448

❑ Phone: (812) 988-2355 or (812) 988-2308

❑ Hours: Daily 10:00am-8:00pm (April-October)

❑ Admission: $4.00 (ages 5+)

❑ Tours: 2.5 mile narrated tour of downtown. Pickup at major motels every 30 minutes.

Simulated steam locomotive train offers a 2.5-mile narrated tour of downtown Nashville.

T.C. STEELE STATE HISTORIC SITE

4220 South T.C Steele Road (1.5 miles south of Hwy 46 at Belmont, off SR 4)

Nashville 47448

❑ Phone: (812) 988-2785

www.browncountystatepark.com/indiana/steele.html

❑ Hours: Tuesday-Saturday 9:00am-5:00pm, Sunday 1:00-5:00pm (mid December-mid March). Closed Thanksgiving, Christmastime, New Years and Easter.

❑ Admission: FREE, donations accepted.

The site is Theodore Clement Steele's (1847-1926), a noted Indiana artist's, home and studio. See exhibits of Impressionistic paintings by the Hoosier Group painter. Surrounding nature preserves provide inspiration. Guided tours are offered through "The House of the Singing Winds" and the Large Studio where changing exhibits display paintings done throughout Steele's life. The 211-acre site includes four hiking trails, the Dewar Log Cabin and the 92-acre Selma Steele Nature Preserve.

YELLOWWOOD STATE FOREST

772 South Yellowwood Road (7 miles west of Nashville off State Highway 46 (Follow signs from 46.)

Nashville 47448

❑ Phone: (812) 988-7945, **Web: www.in.gov/dnr/forestry/**

Yellowwood offers 23,400 wooded acres with three primitive lakes, camping, biking, horse and hiking trails, nature study, fishing, and boat rental. Panning for gold is permitted on Morgan-Monroe and Yellowwood State Forests. A gold panning permit is required. The permit, which can be obtained free of charge, allows for panning gold on a hobby basis. Yellowwood State Forest is named for a tree common in the mid-south but rare this far north.

The yellowwood tree (Cladrastis kentukea) has bright yellow heartwood that is hard and dense. The tree flowers abundantly but only every three to five years in the spring with loose clusters of pea-like, fragrant white flowers. Less than 200 acres in Yellowwood support the yellowwood tree on north facing slopes and deep ravines near Crooked Creek Lake.

CANTERBURY ARABIANS

12131 East 196th Street

Noblesville 46060

❑ Phone: (317) 776-0779
❑ Hours: Daily 8:00am-5:00pm (call first)
❑ Admission: FREE
❑ Tours: By appointment

Visit with "Real Mac" – a former Indianapolis Colt's Mascot. Lovers of Arabians get to visit a real working horse farm. See bathing, eating, or a foal being born. Best visiting time is Spring/Summer when new colts arrive.

HAMILTON COUNTY THEATRE/ BELFRY THEATRE

SR 238

Noblesville 46060

❑ Phone: (317) 773-0398, **Web: www.hctg.org**
❑ Season: (September-July)
❑ Admission: $8.00-$10.00

Enjoy theatrical productions like "Charlottes Web" and "Charlie Brown". One of Indiana's oldest and most honored community theaters, the company produces six family-oriented comedies, dramas, and musicals annually.

INDIANA TRANSPORTATION MUSEUM

325 Cicero Road (1 mile north of State Route 32 on State Route 19, North and West of downtown Noblesville)

Noblesville (Forest Park) 46060

❑ Phone: (317) 773-6000, **Web:** www.itm.org
❑ Hours: Tuesday-Sunday 10:00am-5:00pm (Memorial Day-Labor Day). Weekends only (April, May, September, October).
❑ Admission: Museum only: $2.00-$3.00 (age 3+). Train rides (includes museum): $8.50-$12.00 adult, $5.50-$8.00 child.

Ride to the Indiana State Fair or just a simple tour on an authentic steam or diesel train. Tour 50 rail cars with antics and stories from retired railroad volunteers. Artifacts are displayed within train cars. The private rolling hotel suite of millionaire Henry Flagler can be toured on special holidays. Trolley rides are available daily during the season, and train rides are available on weekends only. The Weekend Train runs on the main line, from Hobbs Station located at the Museum, on Saturdays and Sundays (except during Fairtrain in August). The Tipton Pizza Train takes families to a pizza buffet in Tipton on alternate Fridays.

GROVER MUSEUM/ SHELBY COUNTY MUSEUM

52 W. Broadway (I-74 Shelbyville exit and head south on State Road 9), **Shelbyville** 46176

❑ Phone: (317) 392-4634, **Web:** www.grovermuseum.org
❑ Hours: Tuesday-Saturday 10:00am-4:00pm. Closed holidays.
❑ Admission: FREE, donations accepted.

Three changing galleries including a permanent Model Railroad Layout and a walk-thru Street Scene with 28 buildings in 1900-1910 decor with Shelby County artifacts.

Each room or store is representative of all the parts of an early 20th century community. Fun way to study local history.

APPLEWORKS FARM

CR 250W (I-65 North to US 31North to CR250 W (south)

Trafalgar 46181

❑   Phone: (317) 878-9317 or (317) 736-0309 tours
Web: www.apple-works.com
❑   Admission: $2.50-$4.50 per person depending on number of activities on tour and whether or not a snack is included.
❑   Tours: Pre-scheduled group tours on weekdays. In case of inclement weather, the tours are provided mostly indoors. No rainchecks.

This farm prides themselves in introducing kids to the joys of science and nature in their orchard and barn tours. They host field trips in the spring and fall.

❑   SPRING FIELD TRIPS: kids enjoy a tour of the greenhouse and do some fun hands-on activities, including planting their own seeds, which they can take home to watch them grow. If your scheduled field trip coincides with bloom, they will take you on a tour through the orchard to watch the bees. (hard to schedule as mother nature can vary by as much as two weeks earlier or later than average. Check around mid-April for an update).

❑   FALL FIELD TRIPS: begin in the barn with a talk about apples, taking into consideration the ages of your children. Kids sample a sweet apple and a tart apple to experience the differences in apple flavors and see a number of apples to observe their variety in shape and color. The next stop is the glass beehive where children learn about the importance of the honeybee and pollination. Classes also get to tour the chill room, see the apple washing machine and a modern continuous cider press and UV pasteurization system as well as seeing the kitchen where they prepare delicious fruit filled desserts. If weather permits, children take a tractor drawn wagon ride through the orchard where they can pick their own apple. Later in October, children also have the option of picking a pumpkin. Children also get to visit the petting zoo and spend some time with the animals.

SUGGESTED LODGING AND DINING

COMFORT INN WEST, **Indianapolis**. 5855 Rockville Road, 317-487-9800 or **www.comfortinn.com/hotel/in428**. The first hotel, ever, to meet all of our family-friendly criteria. Start with spacious rooms and many in-room amenities. Now, add a free deluxe continental breakfast, a fitness room, a playroom with ball pit and arcade games, and an adjoining indoor tropical atrium pool. Top it all off with a popcorn cart available on some evenings. They also have a "Family Value" attraction value package and family-friendly prices!

MAYBERRY CAFÉ, **Danville** (20 miles west of Indy). 78 West Main Street (US 36 west). (317) 745-4067. They have a new upstairs and a remodeled downstairs. The trip into TV Land starts with Barney's Patrol Car parked out front! As soon as you walk in, you're transformed back to a diner cafe where home-cooked food is served. Many entrees are named after Andy, Opie, Barney, Emmett or maybe Floyd. Aunt Bea says, "If you finish your plate - you get dessert". Each child receives a token redeemable for one toy from Opie's Toy chest or one Opie Sundae. Andy Griffith reruns are played on TV's throughout the diner. Don't miss the autographed photos of the stars displayed throughout the site. Goober Hat Night is every Tuesday. Wear a hat and enter a drawing to win a free dinner. If you're lucky enough to get a table upstairs, ask to use the dumb waiter/elevator to go up! There's a varied kid's menu with a mini etch-a-sketch to play with while you wait for your order. By far, one of our favorite "theme" restaurants. Moderate prices. Daily 11:00am-9:30pm or 10:00pm.

JILLIANS, **Indianapolis**. 141 S. Meridian St, 317-822-9300 or **www.jillians.com**. For fun and games and classic American food favorites. Our son, Daniel, hit many a big ticket score at Skeeball. Try to leave before 9:00pm as that's when it becomes more of an entertainment venue for adults. By the way, they even have bowling...upstairs.

CROWNE PLAZA HOTEL at Historic Union Station, **Indianapolis**. 123 West Louisiana Street, 317-631-2221 or **www.crowneplaza.com/ind-downtown**. An active Amtrak station still runs above. Listen for a muffled rumbling or subtle vibration of a train as it rolls through the building. Look for white fiberglass ghost travelers dressed in early 1900's clothing still lovingly lingering about the premises. If you want to spend the night downtown, try a Pullman Train Car sleep room. Amenities include: indoor pool, whirlpool, restaurant and the Circle Center mall food court just a block away.

BAZBEAUX PIZZA, **Indianapolis**, Downtown Art & Theatre District or Broad Ripple Village. (317) 636-7662. This is an eclectic area with like food. Try an unusual gourmet pizza or maybe a Muffaletta (olive relish...humm - never had it before, don't like olives - but it was good!) or Popeye sandwich. Just their names sound fun. Lunch and dinner.

BRICKYARD CROSSING GOLF RESORT & INN, **Indianapolis** (Speedway). **www.brickyardcrossing.com**. Located on the grounds of the Speedway! The comfortable hotel has an outdoor swimming pool and the Brickyard Restaurant where you might "bump" into a famous driver or just hang out with other enthusiastic race fans. The Children's Menu has average prices around $3.00.

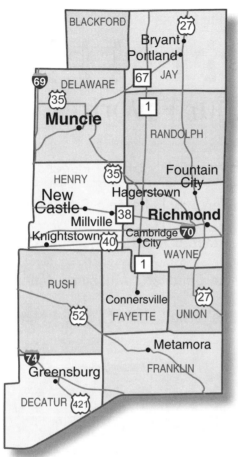

Chapter 2
Central East Area - (CE)

Our Favorites...

* Abbott's Candy Shop - Hagerstown

* Whitewater Canal Historic Site - Metamora

* National Model Aviation Museum - Muncie

* Muncie Children's Museum - Muncie

* Indiana Basketball Hall of Fame - New Castle

Models, Models, of all kinds...

BROOKVILLE LAKE STATE RESERVOIR

US 27 to SR 101 South

Brookville 47012

❑ Phone: (765) 647-2657
   www.in.gov/dnr/parklake/reservoirs/brookville.html
❑ Admission: $4.00-$5.00 per vehicle.
❑ Miscellaneous: Whitewater Memorial State Park nearby
   has emptied their water basin but still has "land lover"
   activities such as bridle trails and picnicking.

The Lake is situated in the picturesque Whitewater River Valley.
Whitewater rafting is king here, April-October. Recreational
activities include: Archery Range, Boating / 9 Launch Ramps,
Camping, Cultural Arts Programs, Fishing/Ice Fishing, Hiking
Trails, Horseshoe pits, Interpretive / Recreational Programs,
Marina, Swimming/2 Beaches, and Volleyball.

BEARCREEK FARMS

8341 North 400 East (Off US 27)

Bryant 47326

❑ Phone: (260) 997-6822 or (800) 288-7630
   Web: www.bearcreekfarms.com
❑ Showtimes for Theatre: Tuesday-Saturday 2:00pm &
   7:30pm, Sunday at 2:00pm. (April-December). Resort
   open daily from March to December. Some shops and
   museum open Mid-April thru October.
❑ Admission: Resort grounds - FREE. Shows are $10.00
   adult, $5.00 child. Family Day Sunday all shows are $8.00
   per person. Lodging is moderately priced.
❑ Miscellaneous: Christmas themed shows run November till
   Christmastime. Additional Saturday Show at 9:15pm.

If you're in town or spending the night at one of their country
cabins on the property, you'll have a variety of activities to

choose from depending on the season (check their website for seasonal packages). The Ole Swimming Hole indoor pool has twisty waterslides for all ages and Indoor mini-golf (sm. Fee). The Goodtime Theatre features live high energy musical performances filled with theatrical themes like country, the 50's or Patriotism. The Tin Lizzy Museum is a place where you can enjoy a tribute to Henry Ford and his contribution to the industrial revolution. While visiting Bearcreek Farms Country Resort do not forget to visit the Homestead Restaurant (open daily for lunch and dinner) and numerous gift shops.

HUDDLESTON FARMHOUSE MUSEUM

838 National Road (US 40 West)

Cambridge City 47327

- ❏ Phone: (765) 478-3172
  Web: www.historiclandmarks.org/what/huddleston.html
- ❏ Hours: Wednesday-Saturday 10:00am-3:30pm (Year round - except January).
- ❏ Admission: $3.00-$5.00 (age 6+).
- ❏ Tours: Guided tours every half hour.
- ❏ Miscellaneous: Theme days like Dairy Days and Harvest Supper plus many historical re-enactments.

Experience the life of an early pioneer farming family who opened their home to travelers for meals, provisions, shelter and feed/rest for horses. John and Susannah's home was built between 1839 and 1841 and includes a restored barn, three-story farmhouse, a springhouse and smokehouse. Many of the family's personal possessions like wooden bowls and special occasion parlor chairs, plus essentials for eleven children are displayed. Our favorite part of the tour was the basement where the Huddleston's apparently rented-out two "travelers' kitchens" used for cooking and sleeping.

WHITEWATER VALLEY RAILROAD

300 S Eastern Avenue (Downtown)
Connersville 47331

❑ Phone: (765) 825-2054
Web: www.whitewatervalleyrr.org
❑ Hours: Saturdays, Sundays, Holidays at Noon (May-October) EST.
❑ Admission: $16.00 adult, $9.00 child (2-12)
❑ Tours: Start at Noon. 2 hour stop, returns at 5:00pm. Early train (10:00 am) in October (Thursday & Friday).
❑ Miscellaneous: Bring a sack lunch to eat while on the train. Sit-down meals in stop at Metamora. Gift Shop with extensive "Thomas The Train" items.

Indiana's Longest Scenic Railroad provides a 32 mile round trip on a historic locomotive #25. The railroad operates other historically significant diesel locomotives and open window coaches on a regular schedule, from Connersville to Metamora. Another WVRR train comprised of a locomotive and one or two coaches operates as the Metamora Shuttle, carrying passengers further South on a two-mile excursion along the restored canal, past the Canal Boat dock, a working aqueduct, and a restored lock. There are vintage Stillwell open window coaches and a restored woodside caboose that ride along the Whitewater River past dams, gristmills and the canal tow path. Great way to spend the day with family and stop over in the fun town of Metamora!

LEVI COFFIN HOUSE STATE HISTORIC HOUSE

113 US 27 (6 miles North of I-70 - Exit 151)

Fountain City 47341

❑ Phone: (765) 847-2432

www.in.gov/ism/HistoricSites/LeviCoffin/Historic.asp

❑ Hours: Tuesday-Saturday 1:00-4:00pm (June-August). Saturday only, 1:00-4:00pm (September-October)

❑ Admission: Average $2.00 per person (age 6+).

❑ Tours: Pre-scheduled school group discounts and tours.

Owned by the Coffins, this was an eight room refuge and rest home for slaves (up to 2000 total) on their escape North. The stop was part of the Underground Railroad so named because it was a secret stop between destinations. Some would stay a few days and others weeks until they felt well enough to travel on. You'll get to see the second floor hiding place. The owners, Levi and Catharine are characterized as Simeon and Rachael Halliday in the story "Uncle Tom's Cabin". This stop was so successful that all of the slaves who stopped here eventually reached freedom. What does the number of roses in a vase in the front window symbolize?

ABBOTT'S CANDY SHOP

48 East Walnut (I-70 to north SR 1 to SR 38 [Left] to Perry [Left] to Walnut [Right])

Hagerstown 47346

❑ Phone: (765) 489-4442, **Web: www.abbottscandy.com**

❑ Hours: Candy Shop: Monday-Friday 9:00am-5:00pm. Also open Saturdays 9:00am-5:00pm during Winter Holiday Season. Observation area within shop is open when store is open. No reserved tour required for caramel observation kitchen.

For updates, visit our website: www.KidsLoveTravel.com

❑ Admission: FREE

❑ Tours: Except Thanksgiving - Christmas. By appointment. 3rd grade+. Best before 11:30am, not Lunch time. Fee.

❑ Miscellaneous: First visit entitles you to one free sample of caramel wrapped right off the line.

Founded in the 1890's and still owned by the Abbott family members, they are nationally famous for their homemade caramels and chocolates made from 100-year-old recipes. See the caramels made from scratch. First, butter is boiled in copper kettles and then milk and sugar are added. It was fun to hear the cook yell "CARAMEL!" just at the time it's finished cooking. The other ladies hurry over to help pour out the hot mixture on cold marble slabs. After it cools, the caramels are cut using a hand crank and each morsel is wrapped individually in white wax paper or sent over to the chocolate room. After leaving the kitchen, the tour moves into the "chocolate room" where the various centers are coated with chocolate. Cream centers are formed by hand or by using dies and a hand press. Caramels that are to be covered in chocolate are specially cut to size and the various nut and caramel clusters are made in the kitchen using a large depositor to drop hot caramel onto beds of nutmeats. You'll love their line of funny-named candies called Gismo, Gisnut, Gishew and Gismond. Can you guess which nut belongs in each candy?

CARTHAGE, KNIGHTSTOWN AND SHIRLEY RAILROAD TRAIN

112 West Carey Street (I-70 to SR 109 Exit South Downtown)

Knightstown 46148

❑ Phone: (765) 345-5561 or (800) 345-2704
Web: http://cksrailroad.homestead.com/TrainRides.html

❑ Hours: Friday-Sunday & Holidays 10:30am-4:30pm (May-October).

Carthage, Knightstown & Shirley Railroad Train *(cont.)*

❏   Admission: $7.00 adult, $5.00 child (3-11)
❏   Tours: 1 hour, 15 minutes round trip. Departure at 11:00
     am, 1:00 & 3:00 pm on Saturday & Sunday & Holidays.
     Only departure 11:00am on Fridays.
❏   Miscellaneous: Quick stop in Carthage for a snack. Group
     rates 20+. Train Robbery trips in May, June and August.
     Gift Shop.

Sit in the coach or caboose as it heads south passing under a
railroad bridge and through the countryside ranging from
cornfields to woodland ravines, past the Big Blue River or a
working sawmill. The covered platform car (once part of a
New York Central passenger and freight station) serves as a
spot to ride those in strollers or wheelchairs. As the engine
is "run around" for the return trip, you can view rail
equipment displays as you get off to stretch you legs.

WHITEWATER CANAL STATE HISTORIC SITE

19083 Clayborn Street (8 miles West of Brookville, US 52)

Metamora 47030

❏   Phone: (765) 647-6512
     www.ai.org/ism/HistoricSites/WhitewaterCanal/historic.asp
❏   Hours: Wednesday-Saturday 9:00am-5:00pm (April to
     mid-December). Closed Thanksgiving, Christmastime,
     New Years and Easter.
❏   Admission: FREE
❏   Tours: 30 Minute Canal boat tour, $1.00 /person. Tuesday-
     Sunday 1:00-4:00pm (May-October).
❏   Miscellaneous: Gristmill on site grinds grain for purchase.

Originally a town built around the canal between 1836-1847.
Visitors can step back in time while taking a leisurely 25-

minute cruise on the Ben Franklin III. Along the route they pass the Duck Creek Aqueduct, a covered bridge that carries the canal 16 feet over Duck Creek. It is believed to be the only structure of its kind in the nation. After the canal transportation era ended, the canal was used as a source of water power for many grist mills. The Metamora Grist Mill is an example. It is still in operation, producing meal and flour, much as it did nearly 50 years ago. Hundreds of cute little shops (they made the stores very small, scaled down, mini-village look). This is a full day excursion - if you don't mind crowds, we especially love all the extra activity and entertainment during festival weekends. Bring a picnic for a lunch along the canal or dine in one of the local eateries.

WILBUR WRIGHT BIRTHPLACE
AND MUSEUM

Wilbur Wright Road, 1525 N CR 750E (just South of US 36 & North of SR 38; I-70 exit 131, follow signs)

Millville 47346

❑ Phone: (765) 332-2495
❑ Hours: Monday-Saturday 10:00am-5:00pm, Sunday 1:00-5:00pm (April-October)
❑ Admission: Small admission per person.
❑ Miscellaneous: Gift Shop. Shelter/picnic area. RC air strip

Wilbur and brother, Orville (born later in Dayton) turned the dream of flight into reality. The interpretive center, built around the replica of the Wright Flyer, provides a look at what the Wright brothers went through to realize their dream. Visitors can read the actual diary of the Wright brothers' father. The home has been reconstructed and restored to its 1860's appearance, and includes some belongs of the Wright family (like baby shoes and toys). This is where Wilbur took his first step as a baby. Learn about intimate facets of their family and faith.

NATIONAL MODEL AVIATION MUSEUM/ACADEMY OF MODEL AERONAUTICS CENTER

5151 East Memorial Drive (I-70 west exit 149B, Route 35 north.
Travel 33 miles to SR 67 East by-pass to Memorial exit)

Memorial Exit), **Muncie** 47302

❑ Phone: (765) 287-1256 or (800) 435-9262
Web: www.modelaircraft.org/museum/index.asp

❑ Hours: Monday-Friday 8:00am-4:30pm, Saturday-Sunday 10:00am-4:00pm. EST. Closed Sundays from Thanksgiving thru Easter. Special holiday hours.

❑ Admission: $2.00 adult, $1.00 child (17 & under). Flying site admission is free.

❑ Tours: Free guided tours of the museum are available Monday through Friday at 2:00pm.

❑ Miscellaneous: Gift Shop with souvenirs plus educational books and kits. National Championships in July and August.

Colorful model planes hang above you as you wander through many well-designed displays that comprise the largest collection of memorabilia and flying models in the world. The types of flying miniature craft include free-flight, indoor, control line (lines connect the model and pilot), radio control and scale models. Look close for the plaques identifying world-record holders. During the summer months, visit the 1,000 acre flying site and see Academy members fly their aircraft in competitions, especially on weekends and during the National Championships in July and August. The fields showcase the only form of aviation open to everyone. We were there for a rocket launch event.... 3 - 2 - 1 ... LIFT OFF! A few moments after lift off, the rocket's parachute floats back to earth. The friendly participants evoke interest in the sport.

MINNETRISTA CULTURE CENTER AND OAKHURST GARDENS

1200 North Minnetrista Parkway (just north of Downtown)

Muncie 47303

❑   Phone: (765) 282-4848 or (800) 4CULTURE
    Web: www.mccoak.org

❑   Hours: Monday-Friday 9:00am-5:30pm, Saturday 9:00am-8:00pm, Sunday 11:00am-5:30pm. Closed Christmas, New Years and Easter.

❑   Admission: $7.00 adult, $6.00 senior, $4.00 student (under 12).

❑   Miscellaneous: Gift shop with educational toys and art. Free Summer outdoor concerts. Saturday Kids Club.

"Minnetrista" means "a gathering place by the water". A series of impressive large columns greet you at the entrance. They are all that remains of the F.C. Ball house destroyed by fire in 1967. The Center's focus is on preserving history through artifacts. What are these artifacts? They are your mother's wedding dress, a Sellers cabinet from Elwood, glass spice jars made by Sneath in Hartford City, or a vase made at Muncie Pottery. They are the diaries kept by your grandmother when she worked in a factory while your grandfather was fighting in World War II. In other words, artifacts tell who people are. Favorite science exhibits usually revolve around lasers, virtual reality, or hologram displays. Explore exhibits on Indiana's sport's history such as The State of the Game: Why Indiana Became Basketball Country. Experience first-hand world class traveling science exhibits like Antarctica and Dinosaurs. Oakhurst Gardens is the home and gardens of elegant Victorian heiress to Ball Corporation canning jars. The Discovery Cabin for the kids is where they can explore nature hands-on.

MUNCIE CHILDREN'S MUSEUM

515 South High Street (off I-69 exit 41 to SR 332, follow signs, adj.
To Convention Center)

Muncie 47305

❑   Phone: (765) 286-1660
Web: www.munciechildrensmuseum.com

❑   Hours: Tuesday-Saturday 10:00am-5:00pm, Sunday 1:00-
5:00pm.

❑   Admission: $6.00 general (ages 1-100 years)

❑   Miscellaneous: Gift Shop. Annual membership available

This hands-on museum is designed to stimulate curiosity and imagination. Older kids may want to head straight upstairs where they can explore senses and weather. Learn about the five senses through interaction with a giant brain, ears, eye, hand, mouth and nose. Also explore Spine Adventure by assembling a life-size skeleton. Learn all about the four seasons, types of clouds and how they are made and experience a tornado with their tornado making machine. In the Outdoor Learning Center experience Indiana from several points of view - a forest treehouse, a farm and pond or a limestone quarry. Younger ones will gravitate indoors again to the dress-up clothes and take the challenge of climbing through giant landscapes or digging for dino bones. Next, they might build a sand castle, play with waterways or pretend to be a storekeeper in a simulated town. Leave enough time for the best display - Garfield. This is the only permanent Garfield display in the world *(could it be here because creator Jim Davis lives in Muncie?)*. The highlight of our trip had to be co-starring in a short Garfield cartoon. For a small fee, you can record this family treasure of members of your family zapped into a Garfield skit and actually interacting with him. As you watch in a monitor, Garfield casually instructs you to jump, dance, stop or run with him. It's a blast!

INDIANA BASKETBALL HALL OF FAME MUSEUM

One Hall of Fame Court (I-70 to SR 3 North Exit, 5 miles)

New Castle 47362

❑ Phone: (765) 529-1891, **Web: www.hoopshall.com**

❑ Hours: Tuesday-Saturday 10:00am-5:00pm, Sunday 1:00-5:00 pm. Closed Thanksgiving, Christmas Eve, Christmas, New Year's Eve, New Year's Day, and Easter.

❑ Admission: $4.00 adult, $2.00 child (5-12)

❑ Tours: 20+ people, reduced rates.

❑ Miscellaneous: Gift Shop. Favorite (and most crowded) time to visit is early Spring for the start of "March Madness".

The Indiana Basketball Hall of Fame Museum captures the essence of "Hoosier Hysteria" and helps explain to the visitor why the game of basketball has a special place in the hearts and minds of folks from this state. The Hall focuses on Indiana high school players and coaches, men and women. On display are signed balls, jerseys and trophies. Visit the MARSH THEATER, where visitors can experience the emotion of the state tournament. Step inside the locker room to hear one of Coach John Wooden's inspirational pep talks. Test your knowledge of basketball trivia on a computer game or pretend you're playing for the winning shot in the final seconds of a game!

SUMMIT LAKE STATE PARK

5993 North Messick Road (Off US 36)

New Castle 47362

❑ Phone: (765) 766-5873.
   Web: www.in.gov/dnr/parklake/parks/summitlake.html

❑ Admission: $4.00-$5.00 per vehicle.

Summit Lake State Park *(cont.)*

An expansive view and good fishing will beckon you to this park with more than 2,550 acres including a large lake. Facilities include 125 Class "A" campsites, 3 boat ramps, a beach bathhouse and 2 large open shelters which can be reserved for family picnics and other events. Summit Lake has an excellent bird watching and wildlife observation area, fishing, boating and rentals and hiking trails.

ME'S ZOO

CR 500 South, 12441 West Randolph (Follow sign 4 miles East on SR 32 to CR 700 East to CR 500)

Parker City 47368

❑ Phone: (765) 468-8559, **Web: www.meszoo.com**
❑ Hours: Tuesday-Thursday, Saturday 10:00am-6:00pm (late April-September)
❑ Admission: Approximately $5.00 per person.

This privately owned zoo has over 32 acres include a petting area and picnic/concession area. Small, fenced-in sections give you a clear view of all the animals. Because it's a "petite zoo", children (ages 2 - 8 years) enjoy it most (not overwhelming). Look for bears, camels, zebras, monkeys, tigers, and exotic talking birds.

HAYES REGIONAL ARBORETUM

801 Elks Road (I-70 Exit 156A west on U.S. 40 approximately 2 miles), **Richmond** 47374

❑ Phone: (765) 962-3745. **Web: www.hayesarboretum.org**
❑ Hours: Tuesday-Saturday 9:00am-5:00pm.
❑ Admission: FREE. $3.00/vehicle for auto tour.

The 355 acre nature preserve with 179 woody plants native to the region, has the 1st solar greenhouse. There are five hiking trails (past wildlife, streams and forest) and snowshoeing in the winter (snowshoes provided). The Old 1833 Dairy Barn Nature Center has exhibits, a gift shop and a bird sanctuary. The Bird Room offers an excellent place to relax and observe our feathered friends....and a few squirrels.

JOSEPH MOORE MUSEUM OF NATURAL HISTORY

Earlham College Campus - US 40 West

Richmond 47374

❑ Phone: (765) 983-1303
   Web: www.earlham.edu/~biol/jmmuseum/index.htm
❑ Hours: Monday, Wednesday, Friday 1:00-4:00pm.
   (September-April). Sunday 1:00 - 5:00pm (all year)
❑ Admission: FREE
❑ Tours: Staffed by students by appointment.

Found here are an Egyptian mummy and pre-historic animals like a mastodon, allosaurus skeletons and fossils. Mammals and birds are displayed in natural habitats typical of Indiana. Hold a LIVE snake! Some highlights include: The Ralph Teetor Planetarium, Indiana Birds of Prey Exhibit, Invertebrate Fossils and Geology Exhibit - displays geological specimens from the local limestone, African Mammal Display, Arthropod Exhibit, Mammal Alcove - displays Indiana mammals in their natural habitat, Marsh Birds Display, Paleontology area - includes skeletons of a mastodon, a giant beaver, a dire wolf, a giant ground sloth, and an allosaurus, and the Discovery Room - with hands-on exhibits that encourage children and adults to touch.

RICHMOND ROOSTERS PROFESSIONAL BASEBALL
201 NW 13th Street (games played at Don McBride Stadium)
Richmond 47374

❏ Phone: (765) 935-PLAY
   Web: www.richmondroosters.com
❏ Hours: Season runs June-August
❏ Admission: $4.00-$8.00 general (age 5+).

Class "A" independent Frontier League. Ice Cream Sundays, Family Fun Nights and Rooster Cookouts are some of their family-friendly promotions. Look for the Rowdy Rooster mascot.

WAYNE COUNTY HISTORICAL MUSEUM
1150 North "A" Street, downtown
Richmond 47374

❏ Phone: (765) 962-5756, **Web: www.wchm.org**
❏ Hours: Tuesday-Friday 9:00am-4:00pm, Saturday-Sunday 1:00-4:00pm.
❏ Admission: $4.00 adult, $2.00 child (5-17).

Collections of Egyptian mummies (laid flat in a clear chest with push-button lighting for an X-ray effect), 1929 Davis airplane, Richmond-made cars and a Woolen desk. There is also a General Store indoors and an Outdoor Pioneer Village (site of many pioneer festivals).

WHITEWATER GORGE PARK
64 Waterfall Road at Brookville Lake (2200 US 40 East)
Richmond 47374

❏ Phone: (765) 983-7275
   Web: www.waynet.org/nonprofit/gorge.htm
❏ Hours: Daily, Dawn to Dusk

❑   Admission: FREE

Fossil collecting with geologic information available to play pretend archaeologists. The Gorge formed during the Ice Age and has many vertical cliffs surrounding Thistlethwaite Falls. The fossils you will find here are from skeletons of animals that lived years ago on the bottom of a warm shallow sea that covered this area. Some of the fossils you may find are clams, snails, corals, trilobites, and many more. Thistlethwaite Falls is a fun place to wade in the water. Walking tours and geological information are available at the Richmond Parks & Recreation Office.

WINCHESTER SPEEDWAY

2556 W SR 32 (I-70 Exit 151 US 27 north (from Richmond) approx 22 miles to SR 32 west 2 1/2 miles)

Winchester 47394

❑   Phone: (765) 584-9701

Web: www.winchesterspeedway.com

USAC sprints, midget and stock cars (NASCAR) on world's fastest ½ mile banked track.

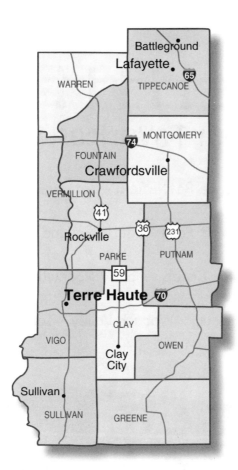

Chapter 3
Central West Area - (CW)

Our Favorites...

* Tippecanoe Battlefield - Battle Ground

* Wolf Park - Battle Ground

* Billie Creek Village - Rockville

* Historic Museum / Wabash Valley - Terre Haute

A Bison & Wolf Challenge at Wolf Park

TIPPECANOE BATTLEFIELD

200 Battle Ground Avenue (SR 43 off I-65, Follow signs)

Battle Ground 47920

❑   Phone: (765) 567-2147

   Web: www.tcha.mus.in.us/battlefield.htm

❑   Hours: Daily, Noon-5:00pm. Closed on Thanksgiving, Christmas, and New Year's. The Tippecanoe Battlefield Museum is closed during the month of January for upkeep and maintenance. Closed Thanksgiving, Christmas, and New Years.

❑   Admission: $3.00 adult, $2.00 senior, $1.00 child (age 4-12)

❑   Miscellaneous: Interpretive Center museum and gift shop. Afternoon Adventure 3rd Saturday of each month - create 1800's crafts, 2:00-4:00 pm. Approximately $20.00 per family. Also, monthly camp-ins, grades 4-6. Picnic/Shelter Grounds. Nature Center open April-October.

A significant spot where (because of the lack of unity between Tecumseh and The Prophet), the American Indian lost his final grip on the Midwest land he had roamed for thousands of years. Also, the same spot served for a rally in May, 1840 when over 30,000 people followed poor roads and trails to sing the praises of "Old Tipp" - General William Henry Harrison who had 28 years earlier bloodily claimed this battle ground for the Territory. The modern, festive political campaigns of today may have originated from the rally where roast beef, pork, stew and bread were served free. Catchy campaign songs capitalized the great presidency slogan, "Tippecanoe and Tyler, too!" as bands, speeches, floats and tales of the battle added flavor to the event. The museum has a fiber optic map detailing moves of soldiers and Indians. Two slide shows in theaters explain the progress of events that led to conflicts fought here. The Battlefield has markers where officers died in battles. Your family leaves this site with a deep appreciation of the causes (right or wrong) of hatred and fame of the men who held their ideals so closely.

WOLF PARK

4012 East 800 North (I-65 exit 178, SR 43 north to SR 225 east to downtown, follow signs)

Battle Ground 47920

❑ Phone: (765) 567-2265, **Web: www.wolfpark.org**

❑ Hours: Tuesday-Sunday and Holidays, 1:00-5:00pm. Best time is weekends. (May-November)

❑ Admission: $5.00-$6.00 adult, $3.00 child (6-13)

❑ Tours: Recommended. Reservations recommended.

❑ Miscellaneous: Special Wolf-Bison presentations on Sundays at 1:00 pm where they challenge each other's herd. Wolf Howl Nights on Saturdays at 7:30pm year-round (also Fridays nights from May-November)... listen to howling, communicating chorus and try to imitate. Weather permitting.

You'll see the herd of bison first as you enter (their faces are so-o-o large!) and then, in another caged area, the foxes (the red fox looks just like Todd from "The Fox and The Hound"). A quarter mile walk takes you and your guide to see the packs of gray wolves in an actual social structure. See them eat (prepared "recycled" animal road kill), quarrel and rest - at a fairly close distance. Learn why the lower class of wolves always get picked on. You won't leave without an authentic chorus of howls from the pack. Even in broad daylight, those calls are very eerie! The coyote is always the loudest - showy! Be sure to try to come on weekends when the special programs (see Miscellaneous above) are featured. *"OW—oool"*.

CLAY CITY POTTERY

510 East 14th Street (Corner of SR 156 South and 14th Street)

Clay City 47841

❑   Phone: (800) 776-2596, **Web: www.claycitypottery.com**
❑   Hours: Monday-Friday 8:30am-4:30pm, Saturday 8:00am-
     Noon. EST
❑   Admission: FREE
❑   Tours: Pre-arranged
❑   Miscellaneous: Pottery Festival 2nd weekend in June.

Table-safe stoneware produced by a pottery factory. Owned by the 4th generation of the Griffith family. They are the only working commercial stoneware potters in Indiana. The hand-jiggered process of molding (pressing out water) is a very interesting manufacturing step; however, the kids seem to like the raw clay best. The large conveyor drying kilns keep things warm - we recommend tours in temperate weather.

SWISS CONNECTION

1363 East County Road 550 South (I70 west to SR 59 south to SR
46 & 59, past that to CR 550 south)

Clay City 47841

❑   Phone: (812) 939-2813
     Web: http://claycity.net/swissconn.html

A "Mom & Pop" dairy and cheese processing facility located on a dairy farm. Tours (w/ advance notice) show the area where the cows are milked, viewing the cows out in the pasture, and window-watching as they make cheese. Even when they are not making cheese, they can explain the process to folks at the store as they look thru the window into the small factory. Sample and purchase Colby, Cheddar and Monterey Jack varieties.

CAGLES MILL LAKE STATE RESERVOIR

1317 West Lieber Road (Lieber State Recreation Area)

Cloverdale 46120

❑ Phone: (765) 795-4576.

Web: www.in.gov/dnr/parklake/reservoirs/caglesmill.html

❑ Admission: $4.00-$5.00 per vehicle.

Most come for the Activity Center and Water Safari Boat Tours. Other facilities include: Sport Courts, Boating, Camping, Cultural Arts Programs, Fishing (handicapped, too), Hiking, Interpretive Programs, Rentals-Boats, Pontoons, Swimming in lake or pool w/waterslide, and Water-skiing.

BEN HUR MUSEUM

(Wallace Avenue & Pike Avenue)

Crawfordsville 47933

❑ Phone: (765) 362-5769, **Web: www.ben-hur.com**

❑ Hours: Wednesday & Saturday 10:00am-4:30pm, Tuesday & Sunday 1:00-4:30pm (Summer). Tuesday - Sunday 1:00-4:30pm (April, May, September, October). Weekends only 1:00-4:30pm (March, November).

❑ Admission: Small (age 6+)

❑ Tours: By appointment year round.

General Lew Wallace built this as his private library and a quiet place where he could write novels such as the famous "Ben Hur." Wallace proposed to write a tale of Jesus Christ, although he knew a novel with Jesus Christ as the protagonist would be a hard sell with the American public. So he decided to tell the tale of Christ through the eyes of a young Jewish noble he would call Judah Ben-Hur. The story would be complete with plots of friendship, betrayal, revenge, love lost, love regained, redemption, and of course a chariot race. He was also an artist, violinist and inventor. Memorabilia include Wallace's roles as a Civil War general, lawyer, state senator, scholar, and artist. A colorful character, he was.

ERNIE PYLE STATE HISTORIC SITE

SR 71 Downtown, 120 Briarwood (1 mile North of US 36)

Dana 47847

❑ Phone: (765) 665-3633

www.in.gov/ism/HistoricSites/ErniePyle/Historic.asp

❑ Hours: Wednesday-Saturday 9:00am-5:00pm, Sunday 1:00-5:00pm. (mid-March to mid-December). Closed Thanksgiving, Christmas Eve, Christmas Day, New Year's Day and Easter.

❑ Admission: FREE

Summed up by a plaque saying, "At this spot, the 77th Infantry Division lost a Buddy, Ernie Pyle, 18 April, 1945". An endearing man who wrote an aviation column for the Washington Daily News and then became a roving reporter traveling the country. He wrote of ordinary people who had a simple story to tell. In 1940, Pyle went to report on the war in Europe and America's involvement. During that assignment, he was shot by a Japanese soldier. The Ernie Pyle State Historic Site consists of the house from the farm where Ernie Pyle was born, which was moved from its rural site to its present location, along with a visitor center constructed from two authentic World War II Quonset huts. The center features a video theater, research library, exhibits and a gift shop.

SHAKAMAK STATE PARK

6265 W. SR 48

Jasonville 47438

❑   Phone: (812) 665-2158.

Web: www.in.gov/dnr/parklake/parks/shakamak.html

❑   Admission: $4.00-$5.00 per vehicle.

Three man-made lakes offer 400 acres of water for fishing and boating while a new family aquatic center provides swimming fun. Now they have the largest and best fishing pier in the state. People of all abilities will be able to enjoy this great fishing facility. About two-thirds of the campsites are in a wooded area, offering cool shade in the summer and beautiful fall colors in autumn. Facilities include: Boating (Electric trolling only), Saddle Barn, Cabins, Camping, Cultural Arts Programs, Fishing / Ice Fishing, Hiking Trails, Nature Center / Interpretive Services, Rental-Paddleboat/ Rowboat, Swimming / Pool / Waterslide, Tennis, and Youth Tent Areas.

IMAGINATION STATION

600 North 4th Street & Cincinnati Streets (Downtown)

Lafayette 47902

❑   Phone: (765) 420-7780

Web: http://users.nlci.com/imagination/

❑   Hours: Friday-Saturday 9:00am-5:00pm. First Thursday of the month 4:00-8:00pm. Scheduled group visits on weekdays.

❑   Admission: $4.00 adult, $3.00 child (3-12)

❑   Miscellaneous: Educational toys gift shop.

A hands-on space, science, engineering and technology museum for kids. See and touch a 1920's fire engine, a butterfly house, a 1910 Maxwell auto or a flight simulator.

Now, pretend you're a pilot or fireman. Other activities involve the Art of Science or Dr. Dino workshops with hands-on creativity focusing on various themes.

COLUMBIAN PARK AND TROPICANOE COVE

1915 Scott Street, SR 38 (downtown, corner of Main & Scott Streets, I-65 exit SR 26)

Lafayette 47905

❑ Phone: (765) 771-SWIM or (765) 771-2220
Web: www.city.lafayette.in.us/park/Cove/Splash/
❑ Hours: Amusement Park and Cove open daily 11:00am-7:00pm (Memorial Day-Labor Day). Zoo open daily (May-October). Park grounds open from sunrise to sunset.
❑ Admission: Zoo - FREE. Pool and rides, $1.00 per ride average. Cove $4.00-6.50 range (highest on weekends).

It's a zoo, amusement park and aquatic center. The zoo has an aviary, "touch of country" petting zoo and an animal house. In the amusement park, you'll find a merry-go-round, train ride and several adult rides. To cool off, rent a paddle boat on the pond or swim in the 77,000 square foot pool with a 160 foot curved waterslide or the kiddie water playground. From the spiraling Banana Peel tube slide to the leisurely Cattail Crick, you're sure to find plenty of cool summertime fun at the Cove. The Frog Pond (actually, a big pool) features a family-friendly zero-depth entry.

TURKEY RUN STATE PARK

Rte. 1, Box 164 (US 41 to SR 47)

Marshall 47859

❑   Phone: (765) 597-2635.

   Web: www.in.gov/dnr/parklake/parks/turkeyrun.html

❑   Admission: $4.00-$5.00 per vehicle.

Turkey Run Inn (765) 597-2211. Accommodations with indoor pool. Rock-walled canyons and gorges along Sugar Creek, Planetarium, Tennis & other Games. You'll marvel at the natural geologic wonders of this beautiful park as you hike along its famous trails. Visit the Colonel Richard Lieber Cabin which commemorates the contributions of the father of Indiana's state park system.

BILLIE CREEK VILLAGE

US 36 East

Rockville 47872

❑   Phone: (765) 569-3430 Village/Inn or (765) 569-0252 store
   Web: www.billiecreek.org

❑   Hours: Generally 9:00 am-5:00 pm. Adjust by season and festival. Call ahead before making final travel plans.

❑   Admission: $3.50 general (age 5+), $3.00 senior.

❑   Miscellaneous: Bed and Breakfast and Modern Inn on premises.

A re-created 20th century village with 38 authentic buildings. As you enter the grounds, you'll pass through one of three covered bridges on the property (this area is well known for its covered bridges!). Stop in and visit a farmstead, a museum, a weaver, a potter, a jeweler or buy an old-fashioned treat ("penny" candy or little Coca-Cola bottles) or toy at the General Store. Demonstrations of the works of a candle-maker, broom-maker, and blacksmith occur throughout the day. Many people enjoy the mule-drawn wagon rides through the village and surrounding area, then feed the animals at the farm.

CECIL M. HARDEN LAKE STATE RESERVOIR

160 S. Raccoon Pkwy. (Raccoon State Recreation Area)

Rockville 47872

❑ Phone: (765) 344-1412

Web: www.in.gov/dnr/parklake/reservoirs/cecil.html

❑ Admission: $4.00-$5.00 per vehicle. Swimming entrance extra.

Like to look for wildflowers, berries, nuts and mushrooms? Surrounded by dozens of species of trees, Harden Lake is a naturalist's delight. Other facilities are: Archery, Basketball Courts, Horseshoe Pits, Volleyball Courts, Camping, Fishing/Ice Fishing, Hiking Trails, Rentals - Fishing Boats /Pontoons, and Swimming / Beach.

OWEN-PUTNAM STATE FOREST

RR Box 214

Spencer 46460

❑ Phone: (812) 829-2462, **Web: www.in.gov/dnr/forestry/**

Hike through some of the best hardwood forests in the country. Enjoy deer, squirrel and turkey hunting. Fish in one of the many ponds. Horseback ride through some of the beautiful hills of south central Indiana, including a view of a 50-foot sandstone bluff. Owen-Putnam State Forest offers 6 miles of mountain bike trails.

MCCORMICK'S CREEK STATE PARK

Route 5, Box 282 (CR 46 near CR 43, along the White River,
14 miles northwest of Bloomington)

Spencer 47460

❑   Phone: (812) 829-2235.

www.in.gov/dnr/parklake/parks/mccormickscreek.html

❑   Admission: $4.00-$5.00 per vehicle.

Canyon Inn   (812) 829-4881 Accommodations, Restaurant and Pool. Unique limestone formations and scenic waterfalls along the White River. Hike through the thick wooded area or roam leisurely through the magnificent canyon surrounded by high cliffs. Also cabins, cultural programs, nature center and camping.

HISTORICAL MUSEUM OF THE WABASH VALLEY

1411 South 6th Street

Terre Haute 47802

❑   Phone: (812) 235-9717

Web: http://web.indstate.edu/community/vchs/home.html

❑   Hours: Tuesday-Sunday 1:00-4:00 pm (February-
December). Craft demonstrations and history films on
Sunday.

❑   Admission: FREE

The recreated General Store, post office, schoolroom, dressmaker's shop, bedroom, parlor, nursery, and toy shop showcase Vigo County history. Terre Haute is the Birthplace of the Coca-Cola bottle. The museum has a large collection of original Coca-Cola artifacts.

TERRE HAUTE CHILDREN'S MUSEUM

523 Wabash Avenue (downtown)

Terre Haute 47807

❑   Phone: (812) 235-5548, **Web: www.cstm.org**
❑   Hours: Tuesday-Saturday 10:00am-5:00pm.
❑   Admission: $3.00-$3.75 per person (age 3+).

This small museum has hands-on science like: a shadow wall, lasers, a stoplight, model trains, holograms, fossils, a TV studio, marble races, a toddler play area and every changing "Slices of Americana" (play pretend).

SHADES STATE PARK

RR 1, Box 72 (about 17 miles southwest of Crawfordsville, off S.R. 47),

Waveland 47989

❑   Phone: (765) 435-2810
    Web: www.in.gov/dnr/parklake/parks/shades.html
❑   Hours: April-October.
❑   Admission: $4.00-$5.00 per vehicle.

A 2200 acre park with Sandstone cliffs and adjacent Pine Hills Nature Preserve. Primitive camping and peaceful hiking trails and canoeing along Sugar Creek.

Chapter 4
North Central Area - (NC)

Our Favorites...

* Bonneyville Mill - Bristol
* Kokomo Opalescent Glass - Kokomo
* Manufacturing Plants - Elkhart, Middlebury
* Deutsch Kase Haus - Middlebury
*Amish Acres - Nappanee
* Circus Hall of Fame - Peru
* College Football Hall of Fame - South Bend
* Northern Indiana Center/History - South Bend
* South Bend Chocolate Company - South Bend

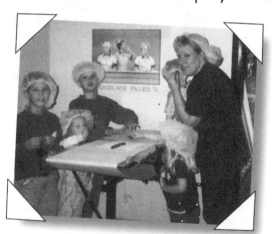

Candy Fun! - Lucy, Ethel & Friends

BONNEYVILLE MILL

53373 CR 131 (2 ½ miles East on SR120 to CR 131 South)

Bristol 46507

❑   Phone: (574) 535-6458
    Web: www.elkhartcountyparks.org
❑   Hours: Daily 10:00am-5:00pm (May-October). Park
    grounds open year round.
❑   Tours: Guided, weekdays, with reservation.
❑   Miscellaneous: Purchase freshly ground grains. Picnic
    area. Milling takes place on the half-hour.

See one of the oldest continually operating rustic gristmills
in Indiana (1832). During the 1880's, milling advanced
rapidly by using new innovations to speed the production of
flour. Many mills were replacing their grist stones with the
recently invented roller mill to grind flour. Bonneyville Mill
never expanded choosing to remain a "traditional" mill of the
civil war era, committed to serving only the local farmers
and a few merchants. Watch as the miller grinds corn, wheat,
buckwheat and rye using heavy milling stones. The freshly
painted red mill and barn /gift shop is a delightful place to
spend lunch. The little Elkhart River offers anglers small-
mouth bass, panfish and stocked rainbow trout throughout
the season. In winter, Bonneyville Mill County Park offers
cross-country skiers miles of challenging terrain and
beautiful scenery making it one of the most popular cross-
country ski areas in the region. The park's two sledding hills
will provide hours of winter fun for the whole family.
Beautiful park and walking trails are in the park, also.

ELKHART COUNTY MUSEUM

SR 120, 304 W. Vistula St. (Rush Memorial Center)

Bristol 46507

- ❑ Phone: (574) 848-4322, **Web: www.elkhartcounty.org**
- ❑ Hours: Tuesday-Friday 10:00am-4:00pm, Sunday 1:00-5:00pm (February-November). EST.
- ❑ Admission: Donations accepted.

13 rooms include a Victorian row house, a one-room school, a train depot, a general store, a dentist, a barber, a pharmacy and a tool room. See one of the earliest toy trains made of cast iron or many authentic Native American tools and housewares.

NATIONAL NEW YORK CENTRAL RAILROAD MUSEUM

721 South Main Street (Right by Amtrak Railroad through town)

Elkhart 46514

- ❑ Phone: (574) 294-3001, **Web: www.nycrrmuseum.org**
- ❑ Hours: Tuesday-Saturday 10:00am-4:00pm, Sunday Noon-4:00 pm.
- ❑ Admission: $1.00-$2.00.

Trace the railroad heritage of Elkhart through photos, videos of New York trains in action and two model railroad layouts in the 1880's Freight House Museum. Outside is a New York Central "Mohawk" steam locomotive that's very dark black and only slightly restored (it looks like it could tell lots of stories). There's also an E-8 Diesel and GG-1 Electric locomotive.

WALTER PIANO COMPANY

25416 CR 6 (between CR 9 and CR 11)

Elkhart 46514

❑ Phone: (574) 266-0615
   Web: www.walterpiano.com/tour.html
❑ Tours: They offer a general tour to walk-ins on Mondays
   at 1:00pm. Otherwise, tours are available to groups of 10
   or more by arrangement. Age 5+ is best.

Their tours generally last about 40 minutes and cover the
complete manufacturing process. View the process on their
website page to preview your visit. Their large piano
showroom is tempting...especially if you're looking to add
musical furniture to your home.

RIVER QUEEN

Bowers Court on St. Joseph's River (Off Jackson Boulevard)

Elkhart 46516

❑ Phone: (574) 295-1179
❑ Hours: Sundays 2:00pm (June-October)
❑ Admission: $4.00-$7.00 per person.

Cruise up the St. Joseph River and learn fascinating facts
about the river's history that dates back to 1841. Children
like watching the ducks and other boats. At one time, the
river was the only method of transportation.

RV / MH HERITAGE MUSEUM

801 Benham Avenue

Elkhart 46516

❑   Phone: (574) 293-2344

   Web: www.rv-mh-hall-of-fame.org/museum.html

❑   Hours: Monday-Friday 9:00am-4:00pm. Open Saturdays (June-August). All other weekends by appointment. EST.

❑   Admission: $3.00 per person, $10.00 per family.

History of RV and Manufactured Housing Industries showcased in the National Hall of Fame, museum and library. See units from 1913-1960's. The units are displayed in a park-like setting with life-size cutouts of characters in period dress. The museum also presents chronological and technological advancements in the industry from before WW I to the present.

GAS CITY I-69 SPEEDWAY

5739 East 500 South (I-69 exit 59)

Gas City 46933

❑   Phone: (765) 674-6135 or (765) 384-7285

   Web: www.gascityi69speedway.com

❑   Hours: Fridays (and some Saturdays) at 7:30pm (April-October)

❑   Admission: $10.00 adult, $5.00 youth (7-15), FREE child (6 and under).

Quarter mile dirt track, racing sprints, modified and street stock.

AUTOMOTIVE HERITAGE MUSEUM

1500 N. Reed Road (US 31 North, within the Johanning Civic Center)

Kokomo 46901

❑   Phone: (765) 454-9999 or (800) 837-0971
     Web: http://co.howard.in.us/johanning/heritage.html

❑   Hours: Daily 10:00am-5:00pm. Closed Thanksgiving, Christmas, New Year's Day.

❑   Admission: $4.00-$5.00 adult/senior. Children under 12, accompanied by adult, are FREE.

The Museum has over 80 antique automobiles and automotive industry artifacts. Many autos, including several locally produced - and the first motorized fire engine can be seen and studied. The Museum also contains a gift shop, presentation theater (seating 108), facade of Elwood Haynes' first home in Kokomo, a replica of the River Side Machine Shop, a 1950's diner, and a 1930's filling station.

COCA-COLA BOTTLING

2305 North Davis Road (US 31 North, left on Morgan Street, right on Davis)

Kokomo 46901

❑   Phone: (765) 457-4421 or (800) 382-8888 (in state)
     www2.coca-cola.com/ourcompany/aboutbottling.html

❑   Admission: FREE plus receive beverage during tour.

❑   Tours: Tuesday and Thursday 10:15am and 1:15pm. Reservations required. Plan your tour and gift shopping to last 45 minutes. Closed holidays.

With thousands of bottling sites across the world, Indiana is lucky to have a family-run factory open for tours to the public. Starting at the bottling line, watch the plastic bottles lined up like soldiers receiving their rations. Keep your eye on one empty bottle as it moves through the filler, capper and labeler machines. It looks like a roller coaster ride as they run along conveyors and then move up and down in waves. They fill 2 liter bottles with a mixture of syrup (secret formula mixed with sweetner) and water plus CO_2 at the rate of almost 100 bottles per minute.

KOKOMO BEACH
802 W. Park Avenue

Kokomo 46901

❑   Phone: (765) 456-7540
    Web: www.cityofkokomo.org/KPRD/KB1.htm
❑   Hours: Monday-Saturday 11:00am-7:00pm, Sunday Noon-7:00pm (summers).
❑   Admission: $4.00-$5.00 per person.

Kokomo Beach is a newer water park. Cool off in the leisure pool or lazy river; test yourself in the competition and lap pool or at sand volleyball. Zip your way down "high-energy" body slides, or watch the little ones at the kids' slides or children's sand playground. A bathhouse, family changing room, and food court make it easy to spend a whole day here.

ELWOOD HAYNES MUSEUM
1915 South Webster Street (off US 31, follow signs)

Kokomo 46902

❑   Phone: (765) 456-7500
❑   Hours: Monday-Saturday 8:00am-4:00pm, Sunday 1:00-5:00pm. Closed Holidays.
❑   Admission: FREE

Haynes' former residence houses many personal possessions and most interesting, his inventions (including 4 vintage Haynes cars). He invented "America's First Car" road tested July 4, 1894 on Pumpkinville Pike. See the first stellite cobalt-based alloy discovered in 1906. While searching for metal to make new tableware, Haynes, in the same process, invented stainless steel. The tarnish-free dinnerware was developed to satisfy Mrs. Haynes' request.

KOKOMO OPALESCENT GLASS COMPANY

1310 South Market Street

Kokomo 46902

❑ Phone: (765) 457-1829 (tours), **Web: www.kog.com**

❑ Admission: FREE

❑ Tours: Wednesday and Friday at 10:00am (except holidays and the month of December) or by appointment. No sandals. Parents must stay with children.

❑ Miscellaneous: Broken glass everywhere so follow guide's instructions carefully. Gift shop. Hot Glass Studio produce a unique range of quality hand blown glass using the world famous Kokomo Opalescent glass.

Dating back to 1888, it is the only remaining "Gas Boom" factory where up to 100 different types of glass are made for stained glass artisans. Four ingredients are used: flint, phosphorus, sand and opal – the combination is a secret known only by the owners. The 2400 degree furnaces run 365 days a year and 13 different roller patterns are used (some are custom to Tiffany glass). The process starts when the table guy rings the bell, the "ladlers" use giant ladles to scoop out different colored molten glass and spoon it onto the table where it's mixed with a giant fork. Next the blob is rolled, slowly cooled and then cut. A pink color is expensive because it contains some 24K gold. Red, orange and yellow are also expensive because they contain arsenic (which is expensive to ventilate during production). This tour is a big *WOW!*

CASS COUNTY CAROUSEL

1208 Riverside Drive

Logansport 46947

❑ Phone: (574) 753-8725
❑ Hours: Daily evenings and weekend afternoons (Summer). Weekends only (September-December).
❑ Admission: 50 cents/ride.

A restored, working Merry-Go-Round of 42 wooden animals hand-carved by Gustav Dentzel (regarded as the finest carousel artist of his kind) in 1896. The Brass Ring, Band Organ and kiddie train add to the fun.

CASS COUNTY MUSEUM

1004 East Market Street (Jerolaman-Long House)

Logansport 46947

❑ Phone: (574) 753-3866
   Web: http://casscountyin.tripod.com
❑ Hours: Tuesday-Saturday 1:00-5:00pm (limited hours in the winter).
❑ Admission: FREE

See how the early citizens of Cass County worked and played in the developing community. You can almost picture Judge Biddle sitting at his desk in the Victorian parlor. Would you like to hear the music box? Upstairs the nursery is filled with toys from long ago and the bathroom is decorated to resemble an old time doctor office. Also, artifacts are displayed on the Civil War and American Indians. There is also a log cabin and barn with period furnishings.

DEUTSCH KASE HAUS

11275 W CR250 North (pronounced "Doytch Case House")

Middlebury 45640

❑ Phone: (574) 825-9511

❑ Hours: Monday-Friday 8:00am-5:00pm. Phone ahead to be sure they are making cheese each day.

❑ Admission: FREE

❑ Tours: View easily through giant windows.

❑ Miscellaneous: Retail shop also open Saturday 8:00 am-3:00 pm. Sample cheeses freshly made.

Making cheese is an art and this cheese haus takes no short cuts. They start with milk brought from Amish farms. The cows were milked the day before and the milk cooled in 10 gallon cans. Once at the cheese factory, the milk is pasteurized and placed in giant tubs where enzymes and flavors are added. Giant rotating stirrers (this is the favorite part to watch) separate the milk into whey and cheese curd. Later, the whey is drawn off and the remaining curd is salted and pressed. Our favorite cheese type they make is World Champion Colby - it really tastes better than any commercial brand (creamier, too!).

AMISH HERITAGE FURNITURE

52886A State Route 13 (I-80/90 take exit 107 onto SR 13 south)

Middlebury 46540

❑ Phone: (574) 825-1185 or (800) 870-2524
   Web: www.ahfurniture.com

❑ Admission: FREE

❑ Tours: Watch production from observation window in back of showroom during operating hours. A 10 minute video plays in the showroom area highlighting the basic process.

Amish Heritage Furniture *(cont.)*

With modern tools, but mostly Amish workmen and women (dressed in their cultural attire), each piece of furniture starts as a pile of pine, cherry or oak boards. They use interlocking pieces (tongue-and-groove) glued together to appear seamless. Now, a craftsman works at his/her bench constructing the piece. Next, it is sanded, stained and hand-rubbed to finish. Try to guess which stage of production each station worker is in?

COACHMEN RV'S

423 North Main Street (SR 13 South)

Middlebury 46540

❑   Phone: (574) 825-5821, **Web: www.coachmenrv.com**
❑   Admission: FREE
❑   Tours: Monday-Friday at 2:45pm. One hour long. Meet at Visitors Center. Not available some holiday weekends. Call ahead.

As you begin the tour, you'll drive up to the chassis storage area (looks like the length of a football field). Now see that chassis built into the familiar Coachmen Dalmatian-logoed RV's. Cranes lift, saws buzz, and workers tediously wire and install equipment. Learn about their "rain booth" that exposes the finished vehicle to storm conditions (reveals any leaks). Seeing the "not so pretty guts" of the vehicle (on tour) is redeemed when you walk around and explore finished RV's available for purchase. Road Trip!

DAS DUTCHMAN ESSENHAUS

240 US 20 (1 mile West of SR 13)

Middlebury 46540

❑   Phone: (574) 825-9471 or (800) 455-9471
    Web: www.essenhaus.com
❑   Hours: Daily 6:00am-8:00 or 9:00pm (except Sunday).
    Farm open 9:00am-7:00pm (Spring-Fall, weather
    permitting). Closed Thanksgiving, Christmas and New
    Years.

Buggy rides along carriage trails and through a covered
bridge are available while you wait for your table. The
Amish Country Decor restaurant complex includes a bakery,
candymakers, and Amish crafts. Kids like the Sunshine Farm
& Mini-golf area (fee for golf) with miniature horses, sheep,
milking goats and baby chickens.

JAYCO RECREATIONAL VEHICLES

58075 SR 13 South (SR 13, just south of US 20)

Middlebury 46540

❑   Phone: (574) 825-5861 (ask for Visitor Center)
    Web: www.jayco.com
❑   Admission: FREE
❑   Tours: Approximately 1 1/2 hours total. Monday-Friday at
    1:30pm. Also at 9:30am (June-August). Closed holidays, 4th
    of July week and week between Christmas and New Years.
❑   Miscellaneous: Groups of 10+ should call for reservations.
    The Visitor Center has historical memorabilia and a gift shop.

Deep in Amish Country, this company employs the work of
mostly Amish and their dedication to quality is evident as
you travel through the factory. Begin the tour watching a
video about the history and production methods of this
company, then, on to the floor where you'll see their towable

travel trailers made from beginning to end. Starting as a tubular steel frame, wood flooring, sidewalls, carpeting, cabinets and appliances are then added. Lots of wood and metal are used and finally the roof is bolted on.

AMISH ACRES

1600 West Market Street (US 6 off SR 19 or I-69 exit US 6 west, follow signs)

Nappanee 46550

❑ Phone: (800) 800-4942 or (574) 773-4188
  Web: www.amishacres.com
❑ Hours: Daily 10:00am-6:00 or 7:00pm (late March-December). Closed Mondays in November & December. Open Friday-Sunday in March.
❑ Admission: Varies with attraction. $8.95-$9.95 adult ($30.00 for theatre show, $15.95 Dinner), $3.95-$4.95 child (ages 4-11). $6.50 for theatre show (age 4-17) or Threshers Dinner.
❑ Miscellaneous: Village shops open until 5:00 pm. Summertime lunches available. The Round Barn Theater "Plain and Fancy" musical comedy about Amish culture and pop culture intertwined. If you've seen this production, check out one of their other off-Broadway productions (shows 10 months per year). Evening shows at 8:00pm, matinees at 2:00pm. See website for schedule.

After you watch a documentary film, tour a 122 year old Amish homestead where the family still clings to simple dress and gentle farming. See chores and crafts of a typical Amish family including gardens, orchards and livestock. The village was restored to historical accuracy by Amish craftsmen. It features a long, narrow farmhouse, a grossdaadi house for the extended family, and attendant outbuildings, all original on site. In addition, eleven restored structures have been brought to Amish Acres from across the county, including a sawmill, an ice house, a mint still, and an authentic Amish blacksmith shop. The newly relocated and restored German School provides another dimension to the interpretation of Amish society by interpreting Amish school. Experience a spelling bee or Red Rover games. Take a buggy ride and countryside tour. You'll have built up your appetite for the Thresher's Dinner at the Restaurant Barn. It's a thirteen item dinner full of family style food (our favorite is the first course including flavored pickles, apple butter and bean soup). If you're trying new foods, order shoo-fly pie for dessert (only if you *LOVE* the taste of molasses).

POTATO CREEK STATE PARK

25601 SR 4

North Liberty 46554

❑   Phone: (574) 656-8186

   www.state.in.us/dnr/parklake/parks/potatocreek.html

❑   Admission: $4.00-$5.00 per vehicle.

3840 acres with beach, boat/bike rental, paved trails, family campground, horseman's campground, general store and nature center and exhibits. A variety of natural habitats await the visitor to this park including the 327 acre Worster Lake, old fields, mature woodlands, restored prairies and diverse wetlands offering opportunities for plant and wildlife observations. Cabins and camping (with reservations), too.

CIRCUS HALL OF FAME

SR 124 (3 miles East of Peru @ Wallace Circus Winter Center, US 31Bus east, right on Main, right on Rt. 19, left on SR 124)

Peru 46970

❑   Phone: (765) 472-7553 or (800) 771-0241

Web: www.circushalloffame.com

❑   Hours: Circus: Monday-Saturday 10:00am-5:00pm, Sunday 1:00-5:00pm (early July to early August). Museum: Daily 9:00am-3:00pm (April-September).

❑   Admission: $10.00 adult, $9.00 senior, $8.00 youth (6-12), FREE (age 3 and under). Museum only $2.50-$5.00.

❑   Miscellaneous: "Summer only" (mid-June to mid-August) performances (twice daily) include calliope concerts, magic circus, animal training and Big Top Circus Shows. Gift Shop.

If you want to see the best of circus life today and days gone-by, you need to go to the source of the most activity in the last 200 years. As you pull up, you'll see the bright Big Top and the sounds of animals and their trainers yelling out commands. In between shows throughout the grounds (see Miscellaneous above), stop over to the Circus Museum. It's located in an old circus barn that served as winter quarters for up to 5 famous traveling shows. Going through the Hall of Fame, you'll recognize greats like Emmett Kelly (classic 1900's clown) and Dan Rice (his act was the character Uncle Sam clown). Our favorites in the museum were the vintage circus wagons, painted colorfully inside and out with closets full of even more brightly colorful costumes.

GRISSOM AIR MUSEUM

US 31 (6500 Hoosier Boulevard next to Grissom Air Reserve Base)

Peru 46970

❑ Phone: (765) 688-2654

Web: www.grissomairmuseum.com

❑ Hours: Tuesday-Sunday 10:00am-4:00pm. Closed late December to mid-February and major Holidays.

❑ Admission: $2.00-$3.00 per person (age 7+). Observation Tower $1.00 per person.

❑ Miscellaneous: Theater. Gift Shop.

The outdoor display includes the B-17 Flying Fortress (as if still on alert on a green English airfield), the sleek, fast B-58 Hustler and the fighter A-10 Warthog - plus 12 more planes. Inside the museum, visitors can sit in the cockpit of a Phantom jet, view a flight trainer, see displays of uniforms, models, survival gear (very interesting), and plane instruments. If weather permits, take the time to climb the tall tower outside and get a "birds-eye" view of the airplanes on display and planes landing and taking off from the base airport.

MIAMI COUNTY MUSEUM

51 North Broadway (Downtown, US 24 and US 31)

Peru 46970

❑ Phone: (765) 473-9183

Web: www.miamicountymuseum.com/museum.html

❑ Hours: Tuesday-Saturday 9:00am-5:00pm

❑ Admission: $2.00 suggested donation.

❑ Tours: By appointment

Miami County history is unique for many reasons: it was the winter quarters for important circus corporations (1880's to 1930's), the Miami Nation of Indiana are headquartered in town, it was a significant site for the Wabash and Erie Canal and the railroads, it has a long military history with the Grissom Air Force Base (now reserve status), and was the birthplace of Cole Porter. The Cole Porter (composer and song writer) hometown tribute contains displays of his Grammy and his 1955 Fleetwood Cadillac. Within the museum are artifacts from a local Drug store, dentist office, penny scales, and quarter player piano.

MISSISSINEWA LAKE STATE RESERVOIR

4763 S. 625E, **Peru** 46970

❑ Phone: (765) 473-6528.

www.state.in.us/dnr/parklake/reservoirs/mississinewa.html

❑ Admission: $4.00-$5.00 per vehicle.

Features include: Basketball Court, Horseshoes, Volleyball, Frisbee Golf Course, Radio Controlled Flying Field, camping, fishing and boating, and a swimming / beach.

MARSHALL COUNTY HISTORICAL MUSEUM

123 N. Michigan Street, **Plymouth** 46563

❑ Phone: (574) 936-2306

www.blueberrycountry.org/attractions/countymuseum.html

❑ Hours: Tuesday-Friday 9:00am-5:00pm, Saturday 10:00am-4:00pm. Closed all county holidays.

❑ Admission: Donations accepted.

Marshall County has a museum located in the historic Lauer Building in downtown Plymouth. The museum serves as a showcase for the county. The main floor is a changing gallery with thematic exhibits. Upstairs, some of the former offices which were occupied by early doctors, lawyers, etc. have been converted to scenarios which depict life in the area between 1870 and 1910. There is a bedroom, kitchen, parlor and a child's bedroom with furnishings of the time periods. You can even visit an old time general store where Mrs. Thayer is purchasing eggs. Other theme rooms include: A woodworking room, complete with a log cabin front; A textile room containing fashions and trim from bygone eras; The agricultural room has the tools of the farmer's trade. Plows, planters and cultivators show how hard it was to "live on the land."; A doctor's office contains all of the essentials of the medical arts; and, another unique room reflects the importance of the church in the lives of the county's residents. A chapel is set up with carved oak pulpit chairs, a portable organ and a handmade communion altar.

FULTON COUNTY MUSEUM AND VILLAGE

37 East 375 North (Tippecanoe River and US 31 North)

Rochester 46975

❑   Phone: (574) 223-4436, **Web: www.icss.net/~fchs**
❑   Hours: Monday-Saturday 9:00am-5:00pm
❑   Admission: FREE
❑   Miscellaneous: Gift Shop. Indian and American apparel and toys.

This county is the "Round Barn Capitol of the World" and a central part of your visit is a restored 1924 round barn museum with farm machinery and tools. The museum also features themed rooms like Homes, Toys, Hospitals, Indians, Transportation, General Stores, Schools and Sports, Military, Recreation, Business, Churches, and the Circus. Each room gives you information on little known facts. Another extra touch is the Living History Village called "Loyal, Indiana" where you walk from the depot to a jail, log cabin, blacksmith shop, stagecoach inn, print shop and windmill & cider mill. The village is only open on Saturdays and during Festivals, except during the summer when it is open when the museum is open.

UNIVERSITY OF NOTRE DAME

111 Eck Visitors Center (located on Notre Dame Avenue)

South Bend 46556

- ❑ Phone: (574) 631-5726, **Web: www.nd.edu/~eckvisit**
- ❑ Hours: Monday-Saturday 8:00am-5:00pm, Sunday 10:00am-5:00pm.
- ❑ Campus Tours: Monday-Friday at 11:00am and 3:00pm during the academic year. Weekdays at 9:00am, 11:00am, 1:00pm and 3:00pm during the summer session.

The official welcome center for the University of Notre Dame is the starting point to begin a walking tour of the mystical campus founded in 1842. A lighted aerial map gives a visual overview of campus, and interactive kiosks allow visitors to take a virtual tour of the campus. Watch the 20 minute DVD highlighting some history and fame, then look for notable landmarks like the Snite Museum of Art, the "Golden Dome", the Grotto and Log Chapel. Be sure to include the "Fighting Irish" football grounds and a snack at "Reckers" (South Hall) food court.

COLLEGE FOOTBALL HALL OF FAME

111 South St. Joseph Street (Downtown, 2 blocks East of Main Street, off US 31 or I-80/90 exit 77)

South Bend 46601

- ❑ Phone: (574) 235-9999, (800) 440 FAME
  Web: www.collegefootball.org
- ❑ Hours: Daily 10:00am-5:00pm. Closed Thanksgiving, Christmas and New Years. Extended hours during weekends of Notre Dame home football games.
- ❑ Admission: $10.00 adult, $7.00 senior (62+) and student (15-college), $4.00 child (6-14). County adult residents are charged only $8.00 admission.

❑   Miscellaneous: Gift shop-logo and autographed items.

The College Football Hall of Fame is designed to put you in the middle of all the action... you'll see the sport from every possible angle.

❑   STADIUM THEATER – 360 degree screen theater that puts you in the middle of a game from pre-game cheers, to playing rough on the field, to the victory celebration. Around the Stadium are Great Moment Kiosks and exhibits relating to the science and equipment used in football.

❑   YOU CALL THE PLAY - a simulated press box gives you the chance to become a sportscaster.

❑   THE LOCKER ROOM - Walk into a scene where coaches are training and motivating future football heroes. Designed to make you feel you're really being coached.

❑   PIGSKIN PAGEANTRY - interactive tribute to the fans, mascots, cheerleaders and marching bands that create the festivity.

❑   HALL OF CHAMPIONS - photos and mementos.

❑   PRACTICE FIELD – Test YOUR football skills at a series of challenges in passing, running, and kicking.

❑   FITNESS CENTER - Test your vertical leap, balance, flexibility and strength on a physical self assessment.

Even as you walk up to the building, your kids will have fun playing on the ½ football field entrance (we bought a College Football Hall of Fame football and later played catch on "the turf" outside). See the "Pursuit of a Dream" (college football theme sculpture - 3 stories tall!) that will be reminiscent for any college grad (can you count the # of pizza boxes?).

HEALTHWORKS! KIDS MUSEUM

111 W. Jefferson, Suite 200 (Toll Road, Notre Dame exit. Head
south on Michigan St/933, veering left as approach downtown. 2nd
Floor Memorial Leighton HealthPlex)

South Bend 46601

❑   Phone: (574) 287-5437
    Web: www.qualityoflife.org/healthworks/
❑   Hours: Tuesday-Friday 9:00am-5:00pm, Saturday Noon-
    5:00pm.
❑   Admission: $5.00 adult, $3.00 child (2-17).

They're putting health habits into play! The center is
designed to help children understand that the choices they
make today will have an impact on the quality of their lives
tomorrow. The museum offers a wide variety of hands-on
exhibit areas unlocking the mysteries of the human body.
When you visit HealthWorks! you will see: Bodyworks!,
The Main Brain (go in to a nine year olds brain!),
MindWorks! Brain challenges, All About Me, Interactive
Learning Theaters and lots of colorful, engaging fun spaces.
There is no start or finish to the floor; you may visit them in
any order at your own pace. Text panels are written at a third
grade reading-level, so younger kids may need some
assistance with directions.

NORTHERN INDIANA CENTER FOR HISTORY

808 West Washington Street (I-80/90 Toll Road, take exit 77 on US
33/Bus 31 into downtown. Turn right onto Washington Street and
go left on Chapin Street. Turn right on Thomas)

South Bend 46601

❑   Phone: (574) 235-9664, **Web: www.centerforhistory.org**
❑   Hours: Tuesday-Saturday 10:00am-5:00pm, Sunday Noon-
    5:00pm. Groups by appointment. Closed all major holidays.

❑   Admission: $5.00-$10.00 adult, $4.00-$8.50 senior (60+),
$3.00-$7.00 child/student (2-17, college) depending on
number of activities.

❑   Tours: Copshaholm, a Victorian mansion of founders of
Oliver Chilled Plow Works and a factory Workers Home
are on or near the premises to tour.

❑   Miscellaneous: Gift Shop - mostly decorative items.
Memberships available.

HISTORY CENTER - Discover legends of the St. Joseph
River valley from explorer LaSalle to industrialist Joseph
Oliver. Explore Notre Dame's history, pick up phones, push
buttons or play a board game of Agronomy. Other
highlights were the All American Girls Baseball League
displaying uniforms of the South Bend Blue Sox along with
actual photos of team members. The "girls" were coached to
be extremely feminine while playing the game (this during
World War II when pro baseball was cancelled due to lack of
male players). See examples of major manufacturing
companies in the area, too (ex. honey, mint production).

KIDS FIRST CHILDREN'S MUSEUM - The large open
room takes children on a trip along St. Joseph's River. From
Native American dwellings (good picture opportunities of
kids sitting in a canoe dressing in costumes, trading furs,
tracking animals or relaxing in a wig-wam. Kids can pretend
to be pioneers in the 1830s in the log cabin that's complete
with a child-sized dining table, chair and bed, plus hands-on
household items. Climbing aboard a Conestoga wagon, they
can make-believe they're journeying cross-country to their
new homestead. An 1838 map of South Bend, McGuffey
Readers and hand-crafted furniture give an authentic feel to
the 1830s one-room schoolhouse. Very creative pretend fun!

SILVER HAWKS BASEBALL

501 West South Street (Coveleski Regional Stadium)

South Bend 46601

- ❑ Phone: (574) 235-9988, **Web: www.silverhawks.com**
- ❑ Season: May-August.
- ❑ Admission: $5.00-$7.00 adult, $3.00 child/senior.

Class "A" baseball team for the Arizona Diamondbacks. Look for Swoop, Kids Club specials, the newer FunZone at the stadium or Fireworks.

SOUTH BEND REGIONAL MUSEUM OF ART

120 South St. Joseph Street (Century Center)

South Bend 46601

- ❑ Phone: (574) 235-9102, **Web: www.sbrma.org**
- ❑ Hours: Tuesday-Friday 11:00am-5:00pm, Saturday-Sunday Noon-5:00pm. Closed major holidays.
- ❑ Admission: $3.00 suggested donation.

An Arts Education Center with classes and galleries focusing on American Art with a regional flare. Mostly regional works with a strong sculpture emphasis. Youth art instruction is offered on Saturdays.

SOUTH BEND SYMPHONY ORCHESTRA

120 West LaSalle (various locations in the area),

South Bend 46601

- ❑ Phone: (574) 239-7788, **Web: www.sbsymphony.org**
- ❑ Miscellaneous: Firefly Festival for the Performing Arts is held each summer (mid-June thru early August) with all kinds of concerts, food and dance to explore - **www.fireflyfestival.com**.

Music lovers can enjoy concerts offering six Masterworks, three POPS!, two family, three chamber and a holiday concert. Side-by-Side Concert showcases gifted high school musicians playing alongside seasoned Symphony veterans.

STUDEBAKER NATIONAL MUSEUM

525 South Main Street (Downtown. Off SR 2 or US 31)

South Bend 46601

❑   Phone: (574) 235-9714 or (888) 391-5600
     Web: www.studebakermuseum.org
❑   Hours: Monday-Saturday 9:00am-5:00pm, Sunday Noon-
     5:00 pm. Closed Mondays (November-March) and Easter,
     Thanksgiving, Christmastime and New Years.
❑   Admission: $6.50 adult, $5.50 senior (60+) and student (over 8).
❑   Miscellaneous: Gift Shop and Science Center Gift Shop. X90
     Hands On Science and Technology Center features pulleys &
     fasteners using principles applicable to vehicle mechanics.

Two Studebaker brothers started supplying wagons to the US Army for the Civil War and then later WWI. Then four brothers formed a company that grew to be the largest wagon factory in the world. Their motto was, "Always give more than you promise". By the 1920's, they were building electric and gasoline-powered automobiles and continued until closing in 1966. (They were the only company that built settlers' wagons all the way up to high performance autos). See the family's Conestoga wagon, a platinum 1934 Bendix and the last car ever made in South Bend. There's also an impressive display of carriages belonging to Presidents Grant, McKinley and Lincoln. The one and only white Packard Predictor is in the entrance enclosed in a temperature-controlled case. Can you guess why it has to be in its own case? NOTE: The New Studebaker National Museum will be: A state-of-the-art building reflecting the design traditions of Studebaker buildings from the '20s and '30s. Located adjacent to the Center for History, on the corner of Chapin and Thomas Streets. Open in late fall of 2005.

EAST RACE WATERWAY

301 South St. Louis Blvd. (along Niles Ave. & Jefferson Blvd.)

South Bend 46615

❑   Phone: (574) 235-9328 or (574) 235-9401
Web: www.sbpark.org/parks/erace.htm
❑   Hours: Weekend afternoons (mid-June thru mid-August).
❑   Admission: Boat rentals range from $2.00-$8.00.
❑   Miscellaneous: Part of a multiple park system that includes playgrounds, picnic facilities, and much more.

A 2000 ft. artificial whitewater course with canoe and kayak national and international races is also open to the public. The first artificial whitewater course in North America is a place where Beginners to Advanced adventurers can ride funyacks for 1 or 2 people or whitewater rafts for 2 to 6 people. Observers can look for the fish ladder with seasonal viewing of Chinook salmon and steelhead trout or walk more than 5 miles of paved and lighted walking/running paths along the St. Joseph River.

POTAWATOMI ZOO

500 South Greenlawn Avenue

South Bend 46615

❑   Phone: (574) 235-9800
Web: www.sbpark.org/zoo/zoo.htm
❑   Hours: Daily 10:00am-4:00pm.
❑   Admission: $3.00-$4.50 per person (age 3+).

The new Huntington Steam Engine has the zoo's future train passengers anticipating their first ride! They have added some animals to their collection, too. The zoo is so excited about a pair of Takin, whose name means gazelle-like ox. These unique mammals are native to the Himalayan Mountains and western China. The bird department has added a female Crested Screamer. The African display is now home to Ankole or Watusi Cattle. Each of their massive horns can grow to be more than 30 inches long. The zoo's female Amur leopard received a two year-old male companion, Nikki. The monkeys have moved nearer the lions. Australia will be hopping as five new kangaroos are introduced to the area.

SOUTH BEND CHOCOLATE COMPANY

3300 West Sample Street (just West of downtown. Off US 31)

South Bend 46619

❑ Phone: (574) 233-2577 or (800) 301-4961
   Web: www.sbchocolate.com

❑ Hours: Chocolate Store & Lobby displays/Self-Tour: Monday-Friday 8:00am-5:00pm or Saturday 8:00am-3:00pm. Closed major holidays.

❑ Admission: FREE

❑ Tours: Factory: By appointment, Monday-Saturday. The free Basic Factory Tour lasts about 20 minutes and features chocolate production and fresh-off-the-line samples. The Inside Scoop Tour ($4.00 for adults, $1.00 for children) lasts about 30 minutes and includes some "chocolate surprises." All tours are scheduled by appointment. Tour group sizes are limited to 10 people.

❑ Miscellaneous: Exhibits and film of chocolate making process in Foyer. Free treat samples at the end of the tour.

From the minute you walk up to the front door, you'll be surrounded with the smell of chocolate (they use cocoa bean shells as mulch in their plant beds outside!). Even the waiting area is fun with "chocolate-related" films playing (i.e. Willie Wonka) and little known facts like cocoa beans were once used as currency. The real fun treat before the tour is to adorn your complimentary white hair net and stand by a scaled-down conveyor just like the one Lucy and Ethel used (their picture with mouthfuls of candy is in the background). You must get a picture of this! The tour is simple and short and includes the "chocolate waterfall" and viewing a 10 lb. candy bar. Look for funny named treats like the DOMER, ROCKNE and NUTS FOR ND. As their sticker says, "You'll be sweeter since you visited South Bend Chocolate Company".

SOUTH BEND MOTOR SPEEDWAY
25698 State Road 2
South Bend 46619

❑   Phone: (574) 287-1704
    Web: www.southbendmotorspeedway.com
❑   Hours: Fridays & Saturdays beginning at 7:00pm
    (qualifying) and 8:00pm (races) (April-September).

Demolition Derby, auto stock racing, formula Indy, classic stock, and IMCA modified.

HANNAH LINDHAL CHILDREN'S MUSEUM
1402 South Main Street (on Lincoln Way, US 33, turn south on Main Street. Cross the RR tracks and 13th Street)
South Bend (Mishawaka) 46544

❑   Phone: (574) 254-4540, **Web: www.hlcm.org**
❑   Hours: Tuesday-Friday 9:00am-4:00pm (during school
    year). Tuesday-Thursday 10:00am-2:00pm (June). Closed
    July and August and all school holidays.
❑   Admission: $0.50-$1.00 per person.
❑   Miscellaneous: Survive Alive! Fire Safety demos with real
    firemen (mornings only).

The theme is "Please Do Touch" and kids' eye-level, hands-on exhibits focus on the geological history of the area from glaciers to the early 1900's. Touch different surfaces that were affected by the glaciers. View Native American artifacts, tools, clothing, and tee-pees. A Japanese theme room (try on an outfit!) and mid-1800's street, too.

OLD WAKARUSA RAILROAD FAMILY TABLE RESTAURANT

66402 SR 19 (Indiana Toll Road to SR 19 South - 13 miles)

Wakarusa 46573

❏ Phone: (574) 862-2714
❏ Hours: Daily, except Monday 11:00 am-Dark. (Railroad: April-December only). Sunday Brunch served, no dinner.
❏ Admission: $5.00 per run for train rides. Moderate prices for meals.

A one and one-half mile ride on a 1/3 replica of the famous General Locomotive past a "mini-village". You'll start by going under an overpass, then past a miniature water tower, over low hills, past a small lake, through a long tunnel and even intersect one stretch of a local street. With everything miniature, it's just the right size for your little ones and s-o-o-o cute to watch and ride! Our kids each got an engineer's cap (pink for girls and blue for boys) which added to the excitement. The Restaurant features Amish country cooking with a bakery and gift shop. While waiting for your train ride, look at the antique tractor display outside.

HOLIDAY RAMBLER & MONACO COACH RV'S

606 Nelsons Pkwy. (Monaco Site) (1722 Mishawaka Road (Holiday Rambler site)

Wakarusa/Elkhart 46573

❑ Phone: (800) 650-7337 (Monaco), www.monacocoach.com or (800) 866-6226 (Rambler), www.holidayrambler.com

❑ Admission: FREE

❑ Tours: Approximately two hours total. Monday-Friday 10:00am and 2:00pm at either location. Closed holidays, week between Christmas and New Years, and first two weeks of July.

Children (at least age 2+, no strollers please) and their adults can visit the factory floor to watch the construction of motorized and towable RV's. Highlights of the frame construction (lightweight, yet durable) including studding, welding, joining, riveting and paneling can be seen.

KOSCIUSKO COUNTY JAIL MUSEUM

121 North Indiana Street (corner of Main & Indiana)

Warsaw 46580

❑ Phone: (574) 269-1078
   Web: http://culture.kconline.com/kchs/

❑ Hours: Thursday-Saturday 9:00am-4:00pm.

❑ Admission: Donation

The white stone building served as a public jail from 1871-1982. Nostalgic items are displayed in renovated jail cells and sheriff's living quarters.

WAGON WHEEL THEATRE

2517 E. Center Street

Warsaw 46580

❑   Phone: (574) 267-8041or (866) 823-2618

Web: www.wagonwheeltheatre.com

Wagon Wheel Theatre is a privately owned theatre-in-the-round that has become one of the most popular summer theatres in the Midwest. From the first summer, in a tent in 1956, to the current 838-seat, air-conditioned building, area theatre-goers have seen In-the-Round stage performances of children's and family productions. During winter months, audiences enjoy popular performing artists.

WARSAW BIBLICAL GARDENS

313 South Buffalo (SR 15 North at Canal Street)

Warsaw 46580

❑   Phone: (574) 267-6419

Web: www.warsawbiblicalgardens.org

❑   Hours: Dawn to dusk (mid-April to mid-October)

❑   Admission: FREE

The largest of five such gardens in the U.S., this offers an oasis of beauty, education, joy, and contemplation for all. It is open to all people, regardless of race, faith, creed or physical capabilities. The ¾ acre garden contains trees, flowers, herbs and plants mentioned in the Bible.

WARSAW CUT GLASS COMPANY

505 S. Detroit Street

Warsaw 46580

❑   Phone: (574) 267-6581 or (574) 269-5166

❑   Hours: Monday-Saturday 9:00am-5:00pm

❑   Admission: FREE

Warsaw Cut Glass Company *(cont.)*

❑   Tours: Of showroom and manufacturing facility during business hours. Watch cutting - 10:00am or 2:00pm (best times if group). No tours November and December.

Using turn-of-the-century machinery, artisans hand cut pieces of clear crystal using techniques of the early 1900's. Stone wheels run with leather belts in a 1911 vintage workshop. You will see flowers and birds appear in the glass right before your eyes.

BILLY SUNDAY HOME

101 Fourth Street (Park Avenue to 12th Street)

Winona Lake 46590

❑   Phone: (574) 268-9888 or (877) 786-3292
❑   Hours: Monday-Saturday 8:00am-5:00pm. Hours do vary seasonally. Please call first.
❑   Admission: $1.00 (Donation)
❑   Tours: By appointment.

Reveals the life of "Ma" and Billy Sunday from the days of his evangelistic crusades to a pro baseball career (uniform and mitt). Listen to a real victrola.

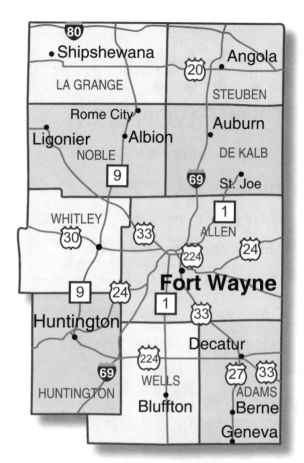

Chapter 5
North East Area - (NE)

Our Favorites...

* Pokagon State Park - Angola

* Foellinger-Freimann Conservatory - Fort Wayne

* Fort Wayne Children's Zoo - Fort Wayne

* Lincoln Museum - Fort Wayne

* Amishville, USA - Geneva

* Menno-Hof - Shipshewana

* Sechler's Fine Pickles - St. Joe

Amish Dressup Tour

BLACK PINE ANIMAL PARK
349 West Albion Road (US 33 to SR9 north)

Albion 46701

❑ Phone: (260) 636-7383

Web: www.blackpineanimalpark.com

❑ Hours: Summers only except special events throughout the year. Tuesday-Saturday 10:00am-4:00pm, Sunday 1:00-4.00pm (summer). Weekends only in May and October. Saturday only in November.

❑ Admission: $4.50-$5.50 (age 3+).

❑ Miscellaneous: Feeding tour on Saturday / Sunday at 4:00 pm is $1.00 additional.

Animals from around the world which are rescued, rehabilitated or have retired from show business are sent here. A unique opportunity to meet (REALLY up-close!) exotic and endangered animals like lions, tigers, chimpanzees, monkeys, bears, and dozens of other mammals, birds, and reptiles from all over the world. Both short and longer, educational tours are available, or, just wander around.

CHAIN O'LAKES STATE PARK
2355 East 75 South (off SR 9)

Albion 46701

❑ Phone: (260) 636-2654

Web: www.in.gov/dnr/parklake/parks/chainolakes.html

❑ Admission: $4.00-$5.00 per vehicle.

Eight connecting lakes are the focus here with boating/canoeing, hiking trails or attending a nature program in the park's "Old Schoolhouse" Nature Center. A beach seasonally provides swimming. Cabins, camping and fishing/ice fishing, too.

SALAMONIE LAKE STATE RESERVOIR

9214 West Lost Bridge West (off Rte. 524 or SR 124)

Andrews 46702

❏ Phone: (260) 468-2125 or (260) 468-2127 Nature Center
❏ Admission: $4.00-$5.00 per vehicle.

Tons of facilities are available here for outdoor adventure: Bridle Trails, Basketball and Volleyball on beach, Cross-country skiing, Snowmobile Trails, Boating & Marina, 246 Modern Campsites, 210 Primitive Campsites, 40 Horsemen's Campsites, Cultural Arts Programs, Fishing, Hiking Trails, Model Airport, Swimming/ Beach, State Forest, and a nicely remodeled Nature Center. The Center has interpretive programs, both indoors and out. The Indiana DNR recently reintroduced river otters into the Salamonie Reservoir area. Wild turkeys have also been reintroduced.

FUN SPOT PARK AND ZOO

2365 North Highway 200 West (Take Exit 150 off I-69)

Angola 46703

❏ Phone: (260) 833-2972 or (888) 534-8421
   Web: www.funspotpark.com
❏ Hours: Daily 10:00am-5:30pm (June-late August)
❏ Admission: $15.00 adult (includes waterslides), $8.00 junior (under 42"), $3.50 general (non-riders), FREE (age 2 and under).

Their rides include: Afterburner (largest in Indiana), Zyklon, Waterslides, Troika, Bayern Kurve, Sea Dragon, Paratrooper, Flying Scooters, Tilt-a-Whirl, Ferris Wheel, Scrambler, Roundup, Merry Go Round, Glass House, Bumper Cars, Go Karts, 12 Kiddie Rides. The zoo has ostrich, lemur, llamas and porcupines! Also mini-golf and arcades.

POKAGON STATE PARK & POTAWATOMI INN RESORT

450 Lane 100, Lake James

Angola 46703

❑ Phone: (260) 833-2012 or (260) 833-1077 Inn
  Web: www.state.in.us/dnr/parklake/parks/pokagon.htm
❑ Admission: $4.00-$5.00 per vehicle.
❑ Miscellaneous: Toboggan Run operating Thanksgiving
  Day through February with track speeds of 35-40 mph.

Potawatomi chiefs named Pokagon originally owned this land. Enjoy this area as Leopold and Simon Pokagon once did. Their Cabin Suites are very Hemingway-esk with knotty pine paneled walls & ceilings, antiqued tables and a "writers table" snuck in the corner. Cozy cut glass and leaf relief fixtures add to the castle-cabin feel. Very spacious rooms with numerous windows and skylights plus a VCR and TVs. Enlarge your space for more extended family by renting attached cabins with adjoining doors. Great place for family reunions (lots of casual nooks around the lodge to read, play games or have a casual café snack)! Besides the game room, video room, craft room (make & take kits), boat rentals, bike trails, snowmobiling, pony rides, spacious indoor pool and spa, and refrigerated toboggans, there's even more to do around the park grounds! Woodland nature trails leave from the lodge and have themes based on what season it is. Their Nature Center is so interesting and every family there on our visit couldn't resist lingering around and around the many unusual or hands-on exhibits. There's even a tinted window so you can see and hear the wildlife outside without disturbing them.

AUBURN-CORD DUESENBERG MUSEUM

1600 S. Wayne Street (I-69 exit SR 8)

Auburn 46706

❑   Phone: (260) 925-1444, **Web: www.acdmuseum.org**
❑   Hours: Daily 9:00am-5:00pm. Closed Thanksgiving, Christmas & New Years.
❑   Admission: $8.00 adult, $5.00 student. Family rates.
❑   Miscellaneous: Duesy gift shop.

America's showcase of classic cars fill the 1930 art deco showrooms of the former Auburn Automobile Company. Some 100 antique, vintage, classic and special-interest cars, from horseless carriages of the 19th century to muscle cars of the present, fill the two floors of the building. Learn how the innovative cars made their mark on our automobile industry.

NATIONAL TRUCK AND AUTOMOTIVE MUSEUM OF THE U.S. (NATMUS)

1000 Gordon M. Buehrig Place (adjacent to Auburn-Cord Museum, I-69 eixt 126)

Auburn 46706

❑   Phone: (260) 925-9100, **Web: www.natmus.org**
❑   Hours: Daily 9:00am-5:00pm. Closed Thanksgiving, Christmas and New Years. Winter hours may vary.
❑   Admission: $7.00 adult, $4.00 students (6-12).

The Museum focuses on post-WWII automobiles, trucks and engines of all years, and automotive toys and models. Over 1,000 automotive exhibits and thousands of toys and models are on display. A special exhibit features 50-year-old vehicles and memorabilia.

PINE LAKE WATER PARK

4640 W. SR 218

Berne 46711

❑   Phone: (260) 334-5649

❑   Hours: Monday-Saturday 10:00am-8:00pm, Sunday Noon-
8:00pm (Memorial Day-Labor Day).

❑   Admission: Yes

Experience a full day of water fun with slides, platforms,
cable ride, paddle boats, beach, volleyball, tennis, basketball
and Concessions. Sand sculpture competition in July.

SWISS HERITAGE VILLAGE

1200 Swiss Way (off 500 South and SR 27. Follow signs)

Berne 46711

❑   Phone: (260) 589-8007, **Web: www.swissheritage.org**

❑   Hours: Saturday 9:00am-4:00 pm. (May). Monday-
Saturday 9:00am-1:00pm (October). Closed (November-
March). By reservation (June-September). Group
reservations weekdays 9:00am-4:00pm (April-May).

❑   Admission: $5.00 adult, $2.50 students (rates include tour).

As you enter the town of Berne, you instantly know it seems
like another country. Almost all of the buildings in town on
SR 27 have a "Swiss look" to their store fronts. The village
has fifteen historic buildings moved to one site. The Mill has
the world's largest cider press. Have you ever wondered
what it would be like to live in a farmhouse where there's no
electricity, central heat or running water? Or what it took to
turn cream into cheese? Maybe you'd like to attend an early
Mennonite Church service or recite your lessons in a one-
room country school? This, and other interesting facts are
presented as you take the living history tours.

OUBACHE STATE PARK

4930 East SR 201

Bluffton 46714

❑   Phone: (260) 824-0926.

Web: www.in.gov/dnr/parklake/parks/ouabache.html

❑   Admission: $4.00-$5.00 per vehicle.

Ouabache is difficult to spell, but easy to pronounce. Simply say "Wabash"...just like the river that forms the southwest boundary for the park. This is the French spelling of an Indian word, so don't be surprised to hear some folks call it o-ba-chee. Kunkel Lake offers excellent fishing. Other facilities include: Bicycle Trails, Boating, Camping, Cross-country Skiing (no rentals), Cultural Arts Programs, Hiking Trails, Naturalist services (seasonal, summer), Rental-Canoe, Paddleboat, Rowboat, Swimming / Pool / Waterslide, and Tennis / Basketball & Sand Volleyball Courts.

FOELLINGER-FREIMANN BOTANICAL CONSERVATORY

1100 South Calhoun Street (near Jefferson Street, downtown)

Fort Wayne 46802

❑   Phone: (260) 427-6440.

Web: www.botanicalconservatory.org

❑   Hours: Monday-Saturday 10:00am-5:00pm, Sunday Noon-4:00pm. Closed Christmas, New Years and Labor Day.

❑   Admission: $4.00 adult, $2.00 child (3-17).

❑   Miscellaneous: Stop in the Tulip Tree Gift Shop that entices you to escape the stone and brick of the city for "gardens under glass".

Even the lobby invites you to a tropical paradise as you browse over your map. Ask the receptionist for the super-duper scavenger hunt and begin in the "Talking Tree" gallery of puzzles, plants, bark, veggies (did you know corn is a fruit?) and a squirting tree. Next, enter the Showcase Garden where seasonal colors are planted amongst clever lawn art. In the Tropical House come and see an orange tree, towering palms or an Ancient Plantosaurus (plants living w/ dinosaurs). Crawl thru the ground like an earthworm and "slide" into the Desert House. Be sure to look for the cute Teddy Bear Cactus. Their showcase display has changing seasons (mums in the Fall, Poinsettias at the Holidays, daffodils in the Spring). Did you know a banana tree bears fruit once and then dies? The best botanical garden for kids!

FORT WAYNE CIVIC THEATRE/ YOUTHTHEATRE

303 East Main Street (5220 Performing Arts Center)

Fort Wayne 46802

❏   Phone: (260) 422-8641or (260) 424-5220 box office or (219) 422-6900, **Web: www.fwcivic.org**

❏   Admission: Average $23.00 adult, Average $19.00 senior, $15.00 youth (2-23).

The Civic Theater performs a wide range of scripts, from Shakespeare to contemporary comedy. Examples are "The Sound of Music" and Christmas-themed plays.

FORT WAYNE MUSEUM OF ART

311 East Main Street

Fort Wayne 46802

❑ Phone: (260) 422-6467, **Web: www.fwmoa.org**
❑ Hours: Tuesday-Saturday 10:00am-5:00pm, Sunday Noon-5:00 pm
❑ Admission: $5.00 adult, $3.00 student, $10.00 family.

Contemporary art. A special hands-on education gallery makes learning about art a fun experience for youngsters.

LINCOLN MUSEUM

200 E. Berry Street (I-69 to SR 14)

Fort Wayne 46802

❑ Phone: (260) 455-3864 **Web: www.thelincolnmuseum.org**
❑ Hours: Tuesday-Saturday 10:00am-5:00pm, Sunday 1:00-5:00pm. Closed New Years Day, Easter, Memorial Day, July 4th, Labor Day, Thanksgiving, Christmas.
❑ Admission: $3.99 adult, $2.99 senior (60+) and child (5-12). Notice your "souvenir" penny change when paying admission. The Museum is open free of charge the first Sunday of each month.
❑ Miscellaneous: Theaters and Museum Shops

The world's largest privately-owned Lincoln collection is based on the theme (in the words of Lincoln), "Most governments have been based, practically, on the denial of equal rights of men. Ours began, by affirming those rights." A wonderfully presented museum, it takes you through the political life of Lincoln and his family. The first thing we were struck by were the numerous pictures / paintings of Lincoln without a beard--can you imagine? Interactive exhibits include the War Department telegraph room (plan Civil War strategies - what would you do?), a touch screen that lets you pretend you're Mr. and Mrs. Lincoln reading mail, or modern day Lincoln Logs (1000's of them) to play with. Favorites are also the display of Lincoln's favorite songs, cake (grab the recipe and try for yourself) and friends. Visitors can see "Lincoln at the Movies," test the accuracy of popular Lincoln legends (he didn't really write the Gettysburg Address on the back of an envelope), send letters to Mr. Lincoln, and cast their votes regarding the past, present and future of America's experiment in government of the people, by the people, and for the people. Look for the rare edition of The Emancipation Proclamation, signed by Lincoln in 1864 in the Civil War Exhibit. A family favorite!

OLD CITY HALL HISTORICAL MUSEUM

302 East Berry Street (Downtown, behind the Lincoln Museum)

Fort Wayne 46802

❑ Phone: (260) 426-2882, **Web: www.fwhistorycenter.com**
❑ Hours: Tuesday-Friday 9:00am-5:00pm, Saturday-Sunday and winters: Noon-5:00pm.
❑ Admission: $3.00-$5.00 (age 5+).

Explore the history of Allen County in the 100 year old sandstone city hall (looks like a castle). Favorites include the 1880's Street of Shops and the 1886 dollhouse. Go back further in time to the 1700's clash of Native Americans and early settlers (see Little Turtle's personal belongings and Anthony Wayne's camp bed). Before you leave, pretend to "do time" in the city jail or take a look at 1900's inventions created in Allen County or Indiana.

CORVETTE CLASSICS

6702 Point Inverness Way (I-69 exit 105B, Illinois Rd., then west on SR 14, then left on Hadley Road)

Fort Wayne 46804

❑   Phone: (260) 436-3444, **Web: www.corvette-classics.com**
❑   Hours: Monday-Saturday 10:00am-5:00pm, Sunday Noon-5:00pm.
❑   Admission: $7.00 per person.

Corvette Classics is a newer museum featuring 51 of the finest restored and judged classic Corvettes of the 50's, 60's, 70's, 80's and 90's.

FORT WAYNE KOMETS

Memorial Coliseum

Fort Wayne 46805

❑   Phone: (260) 483-1111, **Web: www.komets.com**
❑   Season: (October-March)
❑   Admission: $9.00-$18.00 adult, $7.00-$14.00 senior (60+) or student (12+), $4.00-$9.00 child (under 12).

The longest continual running sports franchise in Fort Wayne. United Hockey League. Look for Icy the mascot.

FORT WAYNE WIZARDS

Memorial Stadium (1616 E. Coliseum Blvd.)

Fort Wayne 46805

❑   Phone: (260) 483-1111 (tickets) or (260) 482-6400 (office) **Web: www.wizardsbaseball.com**
❑   Admission: $6.50-$9.00

This professional baseball team is the Class-A affiliate of the San Diego Padres in the Midwest Baseball League. Look for Dinger the Dragon mascot. Promos include Family Days, Dollar Days and Fireworks. Season: April-September.

For updates, visit our website: www.KidsLoveTravel.com

SCIENCE CENTRAL

1950 North Clinton Street (between State and Fourth Sts.)

Fort Wayne 46805

❑ Phone: (260) 424-2400 or (800) 442-6376
Web: www.sciencecentral.org

❑ Hours: Tuesday-Saturday 10:00am-5:00pm, Sunday Noon-5:00 pm. Open Mondays, too (summer & holidays).

❑ Admission: $5.00-$6.00 (AGE 3+).

❑ Miscellaneous: Free Parking. The LaboraSTOREy -- A Store for Science offers merchandise that is fun, educational, affordable and unique!

The science/physics playground is housed in the former electric plant. Kids can bend rainbows, create tornadoes and earthquakes, hold a starfish, or walk like an astronaut over a moonscape where you weigh next to nothing. Here's a breakdown of the exhibit areas:

❑ KIDS CENTRAL - A special area just for kids age 2 through 7 and their grown-ups. Discover more than 20 hands-on exhibits including a puppet theater, a captured shadow room, a giant bubble machine that allows you to actually be inside a bubble, a water table and Fort Discovery - a multi-level play structure.

❑ SWAP SHOP - Kids are encouraged to bring in their treasures from nature and trade them with other objects in the Swap Shop collection.

❑ MEASUREMENT GALLERY - Step into a device that checks your horizontal and vertical body measurements. Or step onto a platform that tells you how many gallons of water are in your body. You can even step under a wave field that will give you your exact height.

Science Central *(cont.)*

❏ OBSERVATION GALLERY - Examine starfish, hermit crabs and other Atlantic Ocean creatures in the Ocean Tidal Pool. Clap into the Echo Tube, launch a wind missile with the Air Cannon, play the piano with your feet, build a self-supporting arch and explore the electrical properties of the human heart.

❏ INVESTIGATION GALLERY - Can you lift yourself into the air using ropes and pulleys? Build a model structure and see what it takes to destroy it. Drop payloads via parachute.

FORT WAYNE PHILHARMONIC

2340 Fairfield Avenue

Fort Wayne 46807

❏ Phone: (260) 456-2224
   Web: www.fortwaynephilharmonic.com

❏ Admission: At any Philharmonic Masterworks, Chamber, Stained Glass or Freimann Series performance, children grades K-12 may attend at no charge with a paid adult admission.

Philharmonic Children's Concerts are presented twice a year in the Embassy Centre and are designed for children of all ages. Presented cooperatively with FAME, these concerts are free of charge. Concert Kids Club is appropriate for Preschool and Elementary children ages 3-7 years who can participate in hands-on art and music activities while their families attend Philharmonic Stained Glass Concerts.

DIEHM WILDLIFE MUSEUM OF NATURAL HISTORY

600 Franke Park Drive,

Fort Wayne 46808

❑ Phone: (260) 427-6708
❑ Hours: Wednesday-Sunday Noon-5:00pm (Late April to mid-October)
❑ Admission: Small (ages 2+)

North American wildlife mounted in natural settings. There are written and audio descriptions of each exhibit. Also, see displays of minerals and gems.

FORT WAYNE CHILDREN'S ZOO

3411 Sherman Blvd (I-69 to Exit 109A - US 33 South)

Fort Wayne 46808

❑ Phone: (260) 427-6800, **Web: www.kidszoo.org**
❑ Hours: Daily 9:00am-5:00pm. (late April to mid-October)
❑ Admission: $7.50 adult, $5.00 senior (60+) and child (2-14). $2-$3.00 rides.
❑ Miscellaneous: Lakeside Gazebo. Endangered Species Carousel, Train Ride, Pony Ride, Safari Ride, Boat Ride (additional fee). Tree Tops Cafe.

This zoo really understands kids and their need to have activity and interaction associated with their learning (i.e. wonderful rides are offered in most areas to enhance the "lifestyle" experience of the land the animal comes from). Enhance learning using globes to orient you to each continent. Ride by animals in a cute safari jeep or dugout canoe or train. Clean and compact enough for kids to easily manage. The Family Farm area has many baby animals and a petting zoo. *(continued on next page)*

Fort Wayne Children's Zoo is one of the top children's zoos in the U.S. and highlighted by:

- **INDONESIAN RAIN FOREST** - Apes, bats, komodo dragon and giant walking sticks.
- **AFRICAN VELDT** - Safari jeep ride on 22 acres of grassland where animals roam free. African village.
- **AUSTRALIAN ADVENTURE** - Meet a wallaby and her Joey. Great Barrier Reef tropical fish in 20,000 gallon aquarium. Australia After Dark fruit bats. Matilda's Fish and Chips. Herbst River Ride dugout canoe tour. Tasmanian devils. Kangaroos. Parakeets.
- **CENTRAL ZOO** - See penguins on parade, beautiful multicolored macaws, the capuchin monkeys on monkey island, and giant tortoises. At Sea Lion Beach you'll see the sea lions as you've never seen them before. Indiana Family Farm area, where you can hug a goat, pet a cow, and see the baby chicks. Kids will enjoy the pony rides and everyone will enjoy a ride on our 1860's miniature train.

FIREFIGHTERS' MUSEUM AND CAFÉ

226 West Washington Blvd.

Fort Wayne 46852

- Phone: (260) 426-0051
  Web: www.jimcat.com/local/jcfire.html
- Hours: Monday-Friday 11:00am-2:00pm
- Admission: Museum is FREE. Café serves lunch.
- Miscellaneous: Just above the Firefighter's Museum is a Cafe where you are surrounded by antique fire engines and firemen's uniforms and tools.

Try a "Life Net" or "Hook and Ladder" sandwich all set in Fort Wayne's old Engine House #3 building. The museum showcases artifacts used by some of the city's earliest heroes - the firefighters. It has preserved the history of the Fort

For updates, visit our website: www.KidsLoveTravel.com

Wayne Fire Department and also gives tours (by appointment) to teach fire safety. Dine among the artifacts in the Café! Say "Hi" to the Dalmatian for us.

WILD WINDS BUFFALO PRESERVE

6975 N. Ray St. (I-80/90 east towards tri-state border. Exit SR 120/827. Follow signs east)

Fremont 46737

❑   Phone: (260) 495-0137

   Web: www.wildwindsbuffalo.com

❑   Hours: Wednesday-Sunday 10:00am-4:00pm.

❑   Tours: Tours available to general public and walk-ins are welcome. $4.00-$6.00 per person for wagon ride tour. Several times daily.

❑   Miscellaneous: The Unique shopping experience for the outdoor lover including: books, music, jewelry, Bison meat products, lunch, or buffalo fiber for spinners, knitters and weavers.

Wild Winds Buffalo Preserve offers a taste of the West right here in the Midwest. The site offers over 400 sacred acres of rolling Indiana Prairie Land, natural Water Ways, Lakes, Birds and home to approximately 200 Bison. Take a tour right into the field with the bison by vehicle or take a scenic property tour by horseback. Tour the preserve on horseback, or use the walking trails. A stay at the bed and breakfast includes the comforts of a pine cabin and a "Buffalo Breakfast." Step back in time and relax. There are no computers or fax machines, TV or public phones to disrupt your experience.

AMISHVILLE USA

844 East 900 South (1-69 to Highway 218 to US 27 - Follow signs
from Berne)

Geneva 46740

❏   Phone: (260) 589-3536, **Web: www.amishville.com**
❏   Hours: Monday-Saturday 9:00am-5:00pm. Sunday 11:00
    am-5:00 pm. Weekends until 8:00pm (April – December).
❏   Tours: Of Amish Home: $3.00 adult, $1.50 child (6-12).
    Buggy rides of farm area, $1.25/person (ages 3+).
❏   Miscellaneous: Gift Shop. Essen Platz (eating place) -
    Amish & Swiss recipes and Country Harvest Buffet
    (moderate pricing, closed Sundays). Working Gristmill on
    premises (can even buy product). Campsites on property
    available.

The tour of an Old Order Amish Home is the highlight of
this visit. The guide includes the children in descriptions of a
typical day - for instance, Sally would go fetch eggs while
Johnny would milk cows or feed horses. A little girl or boy
is chosen from the tour to be the "model" as they are
adorned with different clothes to match their age (i.e. a
young girl always wears her hair in two braids with no bangs
with a bonnet and dress). Pins and occasional buttons are
used in clothing - never shiny zippers. Young brides only
change their outer apron for the wedding. See how families
survive without electricity or plumbing and how close the
families are (grandparents live in a house next to the main
house). Set back on a country road lined with traditional
Amish farms and buggies as people go about their daily
chores. Truly authentic "Amish-cana"!

LIMBERLOST STATE HISTORIC SITE

200 East 6th Street (one block east of US 27)

Geneva 46740

❑ Phone: (260) 368-7428

www.in.gov/ism/HistoricSites/Limberlost/Historic.asp

❑ Hours: Wednesday-Saturday 10:00am-5:00pm, Sunday
1:00-5:00pm (last tour at 4:30pm). Closed Thanksgiving,
Christmastime, New Years and Easter. Closed mid-
December to March.

❑ Admission: FREE, donations accepted.

Stretching for 13,000 acres across the vast forest and
swampland was a legend for its quicksand and unsavory
characters. The swamp received its name from the fate of
Limber Jim Corbus, who went hunting in the swamp and
never returned. When the locals asked where Jim Corbus
was, the familiar cry was "Limber's lost!" To Gene Stratton-
Porter, the swamp was her playground, laboratory and
inspiration. The swamp was the subject of her acclaimed
books and photographs.

GREENFIELD MILLS

1050 East 7560 North

Howe 46746

❑ Phone: (260) 367-2394

❑ Hours: Monday-Friday 7:00am-5:00pm

❑ Tours: By appointment only. Fee for tours is $0.50-$2.00.

A family-owned working mill since 1846. Hydroelectric
generators now provide power to mill soft wheat flour. A
"New Mill" building, just down the road from the "Old
Mill," could produce the same amount of flour in one room
that the old mill produced on four floors. For many years, the
"New Mill" produced flour used to bread Kentucky Fried

Chicken. But after Colonel Sanders' death in the late 1980s, KFC changed its recipe and no longer used the soft winter wheat flour. The "New Mill" now grinds organic buckwheat flour and large amounts of flour for crackers.

DAN QUAYLE CENTER AND MUSEUM

815 Warren Street (I-69 at US 224 or US 24 exit - Downtown corner of Warren and Tipton Streets)

Huntington 46750

❑ Phone: (260) 356-6356, **Web: www.quaylemuseum.org**
❑ Hours: Tuesday-Saturday 10:00am-4:00pm, Sunday 1:00-4:00pm. Closed major holidays.
❑ Admission: Suggested donations $3.00 adult, $1.00 child (7-17).
❑ Miscellaneous: Large screen video presentation. Gift Shop.

America's only Vice-Presidential museum specifically dedicated to J. Danforth Quayle, 44th Vice-President. Trace Quayle's early years growing up in Huntington along with his political career. See his report card from local schools and pictures with Presidents. Exhibits and educational programs focus on the history and politics behind our nation's Vice-Presidents with spotlights on the five Vice-Presidents from Indiana.

FORKS OF THE WABASH HISTORIC PARK

3010 West Park Drive (U524 and SR 9)

Huntington 46750

❑ Phone: (260) 356-1903, **Web: www.historicforks.org**
❑ Hours: Saturday-Sunday 1:00-5:00pm (May-September)
❑ Admission: $1.00-$2.00

After stopping in the Visitor's Center, start your visit of the museum and historical park that tells the story of the relationship between early European settlers and the Miami

For updates, visit our website: www.KidsLoveTravel.com

Indians (lots of trading) and the US Government (treaties). The park includes a log schoolhouse, Nuck family pioneer house of German farmers and most interestingly, the home of Miami Chief Richardville. The chief was considered a skilled negotiator in treaty talks and the wealthiest Native American in North America at his death. Families can take part in their special all-day interactive courses on pioneer crafts, art, archaeology, and more (see web events listings for details).

HUNTINGTON LAKE STATE RESERVOIR
517 North Warren Road (off Rte. 5)
Huntington 46750

❑   Phone: (260) 468-2165
    www.in.gov/dnr/parklake/reservoirs/huntington.html
❑   Admission: $4.00-$5.00 per vehicle

J. Edward Roush Lake. Archery Range, Basketball Courts, Mountain Bike Trail, Horseshoes & Croquet, Model Airport, Volleyball Courts on beach.

INDIANA HISTORIC RADIO MUSEUM
800 Lincolnway South (located at junction of US 6, US 33 and SR 5)
Ligonier 46767

❑   Phone: (260) 894-9000
    Web: http://home.att.net/~indianahistoricalradio/
❑   Hours: Tuesday, Wednesday, Thursday and Saturday
    10:00am-3:00pm (May-October). Saturday only 10:00am-2:00pm (Winter).
❑   Admission: FREE
❑   Tours: Visitors Bureau offers pre-arranged tours of homes, museums and gardens (888) 417 3562.

Tour Indiana's only radio museum featuring over 400 antique radios. Displays feature not only radios from the

20's, 30's, 40's, 50's and 60's, but specialty radios, novelty radios, World War II radios (including one from Nazi Germany), and telegraph keys. Hands on displays allow visitors to try their hand at tuning a radio the 1920's way, by perfectly aligning three knobs.

GENE STRATTON PORTER STATE HISTORIC SITE

1205 Pleasant Point (5 miles west of Kendallville on US 6 and 3 miles north on SR 9), **Rome City** 46784

❑ Phone: (260) 854-3790

www.in.gov/ism/HistoricSites/GeneStrattonPorter/Historic.asp

❑ Hours: Tuesday-Saturday 9:00am-5:00pm, Sunday 1:00-5:00pm. Closed Thanksgiving, Christmastime, New Years and Easter. Closed mid-December to mid-March.

❑ Admission: FREE, donations accepted.

❑ Tours: Guided Cabin Tours on the hour. Last tour @ 4:00pm.

"The Cabin in the Wildflower Woods" lies nestled on the shore of Sylvan Lake, near Rome City, Indiana. It is the second Indiana home of Hoosier author, naturalist, photographer, Gene Stratton Porter. Furnishings in the home are arranged and maintained to reflect -- as authentically as possible -- the Porter's lifestyle. Much of the furniture and personal memorabilia, including Mrs. Porter's library, are preserved at the home. In her lifetime, 1863-1924, Porter authored 12 novels, seven nature books, two books of poetry, children's books and numerous magazine articles. Eight of her novels were produced as motion pictures. Located on beautiful Sylvan lake, you can hike through the woods, stroll through the gardens and rest on a bench under a shade tree...or bring a picnic at the facilities. You can take a cruise on the pontoon boat for a nominal fee. There is access to the lake; however, no boat ramp is provided. Hike a nearby mile–long trail and see the manager's home and barn.

BUGGY LINE TOURS

(SR 5, across from flea market)

Shipshewana 46565

❏ Phone: (888) 44BUGGY

Web: www.buggyline.com/tours.php

❏ Admission: $5.00 per person (ride only). $10.00 - 30 minute tour. $15.00-$20.00 one hour tour. Children 4 and under FREE. Add $10.00-$20.00 for other tours including Threshers Dinner.

❏ Tours: Tuesday, Wednesday, Friday and Saturday. Seasonally. Thresher meal at Amish Home Tuesday & Wed.. Buggy rides (30 min.- One Hour) between 10:00am-4:30pm.

Buggy rides, back roads country tours (in 15 passenger air-conditioned van), step-on guides and Amish farm tours. 1-3 Hour Sight-Seeing Tours or 15 minute rides thru town. On tour, maybe stop at the buggy shop to see what's involved in making a buggy. How about a Loom Shop? Ever think about how long it takes to make a terrific rug or table runner? Of course, you haven't seen anything until you see the Country Store or had an authentic Amish Dinner. While you are touring, you'll hear many stories of the Amish heritage. You are encouraged to ask questions, so that you can understand their way of living better.

MENNO-HOF, MENNONITE-AMISH VISITORS CENTER

510 South Van Buren Street (North of US 20 and SR 5)

Shipshewana 46565

❏ Phone: (260) 768-4117, **Web: www.mennohof.org**

❏ Hours: Monday-Saturday 10:00am-5:00pm. (Adjusted seasonally, especially Winter)

❏ Admission: $5.00 adult, $2.50 child (6-14).

❏ Tours: One hour

Menno-Hof, Mennonite-Amish Visitors Center *(cont.)*

❑   Miscellaneous: Most of the tour is "over the heads" of children twelve years and under; however, you can advise your guide of this and they can accommodate by spending significant time in the Interactive Room.

Where can you take one journey starting in a courtyard in 1525, in Europe, around a water pitcher? Then, get locked in a dungeon, escape in a "cramped quarters" ship, survive a tornado and learn about the power of faith! About halfway through, children will have the chance to walk around and play in an Amish built (beams, pegs and kneebraces only) barn stocked with simple wood toys. Our kids had to be pulled away - we may never buy "gadget" toys again! This is a very thorough walking tour of the story of tragedy and triumph of a people searching for peace. Afterwards, you'll truly understand the reasons for their way of life.

SECHLER'S FINE PICKLES

5686 SR 1 (1-69 North to DuPont Exit to SR 1 North - 20 miles)

St. Joe 46785

❑   Phone: (260) 337-5461or (800) 332-5461
     Web: www.sechlerspickles.com
❑   Admission: FREE
❑   Tours: Monday-Friday 9:00-11:30am & 12:30-2:00pm (April-October). Tours every half hour. Showroom open weekdays until 4:30pm. Saturday 8:30am-Noon. Groups of 6 or more need reservations.
❑   Miscellaneous: Retail showroom has sample table with one of each variety pickle available to taste. Try flavors like jalapeno slices, orange or candied raisin crispies.

Pucker up for pickles! 39 Flavors! (That's pickles, not ice cream, of course) Ralph Sechler began pickle processing in

1921 in his home (next to the factory). Pickles are just cucumbers, salt, water, vinegar and spices but the secret combination prepares just the right taste. Around the side of the building, you might see truckloads of "cukes" arrive (farmers are paid the highest price for "gherkins", the smallest) and sorted into slots for seven different sizes. Each size is processed in covered vats full of salt brine for 2½ months to 1½ years depending upon demand. Before pickles are packaged, they are first cooked for 24 hours, then sliced, chopped or ground and left to marinate 1-10 days in special spice solutions. Workers stand by special stainless steel tables and hand-pack each variety in its special brine. Our favorite flavor is sweet apple cinnamon. Be sure to take some of the 39 varieties home!

SUGGESTED LODGING AND DINING

HOLIDAY INN NORTHWEST HOLIDOME, Fort Wayne

– I-69 exit 109A. (260) 484-7711. Family Fun packages (includes attraction tickets), heated indoor pool, large gameroom and video arcade, 2 story adventure play area w/ space ship, slides, punching bag and roller mazes. Very busy on weekend evenings, but they have live family entertainment on Friday and Saturday nights. Great value for all the fun!

PIZZA JUNCTION - Huntington, 201 Court Street

(between courthouse and railroad tracks). (260) 356-1945. Open daily for lunch and dinner. Located by the railroad tracks in a restored train depot. It's really fun when a train goes past. Actual restored photos of historic buildings around town (like Nick's Kitchen) and the original freight depot. Warm weather dining outside by the tracks. Their subs and soup are great, too.

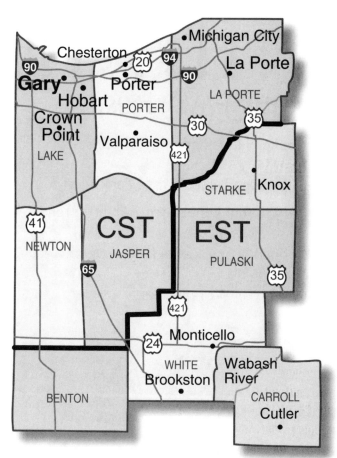

Chapter 6
North West Area - (NW)

Our Favorites...

* Twinrocker Handmade Paper - Brookston

* Indiana Dunes State Park &
   National Lakeshore - Chesterton

* Wabash & Erie Canal Park - Delphi

* Waterparks

Indiana Dunes - An aerobic workout!

TWINROCKER HANDMADE PAPER

100 East Third Street (downtown, by railroad tracks)

Brookston 47923

- ❑ Phone: (765) 563-3119 or (800)757-TWIN
  Web: www.twinrocker.com
- ❑ Hours: Monday-Friday 9:00am-3:00pm
- ❑ Admission: $4.00/person (1-10 people), $3.00/person (11+ people in group), $12.00 family.
- ❑ Tours: By appointment. Ages 3rd grade plus. Open tours at 1:30pm Tuesdays.
- ❑ Miscellaneous: All handmade papers are discounted 25% for the tour group. ("Seconds" are discounted 30 to 50%).

The painstaking, lost art of making sheet paper by hand is back. Twinrocker was among the first hand mills to open in the 70's. Watch "cooked" cotton, husk or linen rag fibers turn into custom paper. Individuals, families, and small and large groups up to 70 are welcome to visit Twinrocker to take a tour of the paper studio. A Twinrocker staff member will speak to your group about the history and practice of this ancient craft while you watch them at work. A tour is 30 to 40 minutes. Visitors are welcome to see the large selection of papers for watercolor, pastel, calligraphy, printmaking, drawing and stationery. You'll see them first beat the fiber with water. We learned this releases cellulose causing fiber and water to bond. Next a mold or sieve is dipped into the vat of pulp and shaken. The new sheet formed is "couched" between pieces of wool felt, pressed and then dried. As the paper dries and water evaporates, the fibers bond closer. A special copywritten exaggerated "Feather" deckle edge is the company signature.

INDIANA DUNES STATE PARK/ NATIONAL LAKESHORE

1600 N 25 E (3 miles East of SR 49, Kemil Road at US 12)

Chesterton 46304

❑   Phone: (219) 926-1952
    www.in.gov/dnr/parklake/parks/indianadunes.html
❑   Hours: Dawn to dusk.
❑   Admission: $4.00-$5.00 per vehicle.
❑   Miscellaneous: Offers swimming, hiking, beach house, concessions, camping, playground equipment and picnic shelters. Nature center has year-round program for all ages

The Nature Center offers a 12 minute video about dunes and surrounding plant life that is helpful to watch before exploring. The largest "live" dune, Mt. Baldy ("live" means it still moves as wind lifts grains of sand & drops them) is guaranteed to make your mouth drop and your eyes open wide. It's a thrill to climb quickly to the top (123 ft.) and let the dune slide you down to the water's edge. (Note to Parents: be ready for an aerobic workout!). On a windy day, place a beach toy on the sand and watch a mini-dune form behind it! On a windy day you can also hear the sand "sing" under your feet – it's true! Another site to visit (esp. during special events) is the Bailly Homestead and Chellberg Farm. Visit the home of one of Porter County's earliest settlers, French-Canadian voyageur and fur trader Joseph Bailly. Nearby is an early 20th century 80-acre working farm established in 1874 by Swedish immigrants Anders and Johanna Kjellberg, who emigrated from Sweden in 1863. (Both properties on Mineral Springs Road, between U.S. Highways 12 and 20, Porter. 219-926-7561, extension 225).

DEEP RIVER WATERPARK

9001 E. US 30 (off I-65), **Crown Point** 46307

❑   Phone: (800) WAV-PARK or (219) 947-7349
    Web: www.deepriverwaterpark.com
❑   Hours: Daily 10:00am-6:00pm (Memorial Day Weekend -
    Labor Day, excluding the last two Monday-Fridays in
    August). Central Time.
❑   Admission: $14.00-$19.00 General, $7.00-$8.00 for child
    (under 46") and spectator. Reduced rates for special night
    tubing and off-peak weekdays.
❑   Miscellaneous: Available for private parties after 6:30PM.

There is a lot to do at this Waterpark including a wave pool,
lazy river, Tube and Body slides, and many adventurous
waterslides like "The Storm" tunnel tube ride. Among the
places to play: the Paddlers' Play Area, which offers low-key
fun for children; and The Dragon, a wild water slide that can
send "sliders" down at speeds up to 35 mph. Bringing a big
group? Consider playing Water Wars, an interactive water
challenge game.

ADAMS MILL

(1/2 mile east of town on Rte. 500 south & 75E - road to mill)

Cutler 46920

❑   Phone: (765) 463-7893
    Web: www.geocities.com/friends_of_adams_mill/
❑   Hours: Weekends 1:00-5:00pm (May-October), 11:00am-
    5:00pm for events (usually held once per month).
❑   Admission: $5.00 family, $2.00 adult, $1.00 child.

A grist mill with hundreds of pioneer life antiques displayed.
A display of "Americana". Most of the original mill
equipment is running. Monthly events are the best time to
visit…especially the Treasure Hunts.

WABASH AND ERIE CANAL PARK CENTER

1030 N. Washington St. (off US 421), **Delphi** 46923

- ❑   Phone: (765) 564-2870
  Web: www.wabashanderiecanal.org
- ❑   Hours: Friday 1:00-4:00pm (warm months only), Saturday 10:00am-4:00pm and Sunday 1:00-4:00pm.
- ❑   Admission: FREE. Donations gladly excepted and used towards running the canal boat replica tour.

In the 1800s, the nation's longest canal, the Wabash and Erie Canal, ran from Toledo, Ohio, to Evansville. Although these waterways have given way to superhighways, this city hasn't forgotten the impact of the canal on American history. The Wabash, which had long been a native thoroughfare servicing the inhabitants of the area, became alive with water traffic and related businesses. Items exported from this area were grain, logs, pork, and whiskey. Numbered among the imports were coffee, salt, manufactured goods, and settlers. Most of the workers were Irish immigrants. Volunteers have brought to life the Wabash and Erie Canal Park Conference and Interpretive Center. The facility's museum galleries include more than 60 exhibits. Everything from dinosaur remains to scaled-down models of a section of the canal and bridge. True historians can hike, bike or walk the 1850s canal, a seven-mile trail system.

FAIR OAKS DAIRY ADVENTURE

856 North 600 East (off I-65 North)

Fair Oaks 47943

- ❑   Phone: (219) 394-2025
  Web: www.fairoaksdairyadventure.com
- ❑   Hours: Monday-Saturday 9:00am-5:00pm. Central Time.
- ❑   Tours: Monday-Friday, 9:00am-2:00pm.

❑   Miscellaneous: The center and tours are FREE but plan on bringing extra money for the dairy bar and take-home purchases.

Want to make milk more exciting to your kids? Take them to the Fair Oaks Dairy Adventure. It's a chance to learn about the dairy industry through interactive displays (meet the cows and learn the goodness of milk), video presentations, and a tour of a modern dairy farm. The "Grass to the Glass" Video Presentation Highlights: Farming and Crop Harvest, Feeding, Calf Taking its First Steps, Milking and Herd Management, Milk Safety and Transportation, Processing and Bottling, Production of Ice Cream, Cheese, Yogurt & Other Dairy Products, and Enjoying Dairy Products. Board a bus and tour a farm to see the feeding, milking and care of dairy cows. Each visitor will understand how the quality of milk is safeguarded and how this leads to the delicious and healthy dairy products we all enjoy. Care for a cheese sandwich and some milk?

WOOD'S HISTORIC GRIST MILL

9410 Old Lincoln Highway (in Deep River County Park)

Hobart 46342

❑   Phone: (219) 769-9030 or (219) 947-1958
❑   Hours: Daily 10:00am-5:00pm (May-October)
❑   Admission: FREE (child 12 and under). $0.50 adult.
❑   Miscellaneous: General Store - old fashioned wooden floors, jars of candy and sundries.

Restored late 1800's mill designed to expose you to the process of a gristmill and pioneer life. Daily demonstrations of grinding corn into meal and the sale of the stone ground cornmeal occur in the mill. Rag rugs are often being made on an antique loom, and the replica General Store beckons visitors back to a time long past. The first floor is where the raw grain is ground by large stones. The other two floors are displays of period settings. Also take a peek in the 1830's sawmill.

STARKE COUNTY HISTORICAL MUSEUM

401 S. Main Street (2 blocks west of US 35)

Knox 46534

❑   Phone: (574) 772-5393
❑   Hours: Tuesday-Friday Noon-4:00pm.
❑   Admission: FREE
❑   Miscellaneous: Annual events include the July 4th Ice Cream Social and a Christmas Open House.

Starke County Historical Museum is quartered in the home of banker, businessman, twice-elected Governor of Indiana, Henry F. Schricker. The museum holds three floors of historical memorabilia including agricultural, military items, clothing, decorative items, toys, a schoolroom and the Schricker Room containing the family's personal collections. Take a guided tour of the house.

BASS LAKE STATE BEACH

5838 SR 10

Knox 47534

❑   Phone: (574) 772-3382 Summer and (219) 946-3213 Winter.
   Web: www.in.gov/dnr/parklake/parks/basslake.html
❑   Admission: $4.00-$5.00 per vehicle.

Located in northwest Indiana, Bass Lake is Indiana's fourth largest natural lake. Swimming and wading are offered, with shaded areas on portions of the swimming beach. A bathhouse provides showers, changing rooms and vending machines. Unlimited power boating is available too.

DOOR PRAIRIE AUTO MUSEUM

2405 Indiana Avenue (1 mile south of town on US 35)

LaPorte 46350

❑   Phone: (219) 326-1337, **Web: www.dpautomuseum.com**
❑   Hours: Tuesday-Saturday 10:00am-4:30pm, Sunday Noon-4:30pm (April-December). Central Time.
❑   Admission: $5.00 adult, $4.00 senior (60+), $3.00 youth (10-18).

The collection covers 100 years - beginning with an example of the world's first car, an 1886 Benz Motor Wagon. There are also Auburn, Bricklin, Citroen, Daimler, Duesenberg, Duryea, Ford, Mercedes, Mitchell, Rolls Royce, Studebaker, Tucker, Winton and many others. The Indiana Room shows a complete set of license plates from 1913 to the present. Also featured are antique toys, historic airplanes, and a walk down main street featuring business store fronts from the 1900's, 1940's and 1960's. Self-guided.

LAPORTE COUNTY MUSEUM

809 State Street (State and Michigan Avenue)

LaPorte 46350

❑   Phone: (219) 326-6808, **Web: www.lapcohistsoc.org**
❑   Hours: Tuesday-Saturday 10:00am-4:30pm
❑   Admission: FREE

With over 80,000 items on display, this museum houses LaPorte County family heirlooms and the W. A. Jones collection of antique firearms and weapons. Kids like the 1920s home settings and the collection of antique dolls.

ABC CHILDREN'S MUSEUM

450 St John Road (Marquette Mall)

Michigan City 46360

❑   Phone: (219) 874-8222
❑   Hours: Wednesday-Friday 1:00-5:00pm, Saturday 10:00am-4:00pm.
❑   Admission: $3.50 adult, $2.50 student.
❑   Tours: By appointment (weekdays)

This Tudor home has 12 exhibit areas. Hands-on, interactive exhibits explore science principles, nature, sounds, music, color, light and culture. Children ages 3 to 10 will enjoy the new "Discovery Town" theme. Explore the travel agency, town factory, fossil dig, puppet treehouse and more.

HESSTON STEAM MUSEUM

313 Kintzele Road (I-94 or I80/90 on SR 39 to east on County. Rd. 1000N)

Michigan City 46360

❑   Phone: (219) 872-5055, **Web: www.hesston.org**
❑   Hours: Weekends Noon-5:00pm (Memorial Day-Labor Day). Sunday only (September-October).
❑   Admission: FREE, except on Labor Day weekend.

Three gauges of steam trains give rides around 155 wooded acres, climbing a grade, crossing several dams, running alongside ponds or dams and depots. Also, steam crane, sawmill, traction engine and threshing machines, power plant and more.

OLD LIGHTHOUSE MUSEUM

Heisman Harbor Road

Michigan City 46360

❑ Phone: (219) 872-6133

Web: www.lapcohistsoc.org/oldlighthouse.htm

❑ Hours: Daily 1:00-4:00pm (except Monday). Closed January and February.

❑ Admission: $2.00 general, $0.50 child (12 and younger)

An original 1858 lighthouse filled with displays of recreated keeper's house, lake lore, ship wrecks, and maritime history. Take the cat walk out to the only operational lighthouse in Indiana. Learn how the lighthouse keeper and his/her family (the most famous keeper was a woman) lived and worked.

WASHINGTON PARK ZOO

115 Lake Shore Drive (On the Lake in Washington Park. Take US 421/Franklin Street North through Michigan City until it dead ends)

Michigan City 46360

❑ Phone: (219) 873-1510

Web: www.emichigancity.com/cityhall/departments/zoo/

❑ Hours: Daily 10:00am-4:00pm (April-October). Open later in the summer.

❑ Admission: $2.00-$4.00 (age 3+).

A 1928 zoo laid out on the side of a wooded sand dune. One of the oldest and largest zoos with a petting area (near the entrance), children's castle, feline house, turtle pond, bobcat/prairie dog display and monkey island. You also can see the Michigan shoreline and Chicago skyline from the observation tower.

INDIANA BEACH AMUSEMENT

5224 East Indiana Beach Road (I-65 to US 24)

Monticello 47960

❑ Phone: (574) 583-4141, **Web: www.indianabeach.com**

❑ Hours: Summer hours 11:00am-11:00pm. (mid May-Labor Day)

❑ Admission: $2.00 general (age 4+) plus Ride Plans $10.00 - $18.00 (or $1.00-2.00 per ride). Waterpark and rides passes combo are $21.00-$27.00.

❑ Miscellaneous: Camp Resort. Free Parking.

The 1400 acre lake with sandy beach provides a day full of entertainment without an excessive entrance fee. Popular amusements are the "Den of Lost Thieves" and "Hoosier Hurricane" or "Corn Ball Express" rides along with Kiddieland, an arcade, mini-golf, and mini-train rides. Indiana Beach thrills visitors with a newer ride: Air Crow. Climb aboard to fly over the waters of Lake Shafer. Riders can swing themselves higher for an even more breathtaking experience. Browse or eat at the Boardwalk and then watch a Water Ski show after you've taken the plunge on the "Big Flush" waterslide in the WaterPark. To relax, try a ride on the "Shafer Queen" paddle wheel boat or watch a live entertainment show.

SPLASH DOWN DUNES WATER PARK

150 East US 20 (1 mile South of The Indiana Dunes State Park)

Porter 46304

❑ Phone: (219) 929-1181

Web: www.splashdowndunes.com

❑ Hours: Daily 10:00am-8:00pm (Summer). Open till 6:00pm (mid-August until Labor Day).

❑ Admission:$13.00-$20.00 range. Children 1 and under free. Lower admission charged after 4:00pm.

❑   Miscellaneous: Gift shop and arcade. Concessions, café.

Giant Twister is a series of 13 slides all twisting by each other; The Tower – Indiana's tallest slide is 68'; Big Wave is the Midwest's largest wave pool; a lazy river; and Sandcastle Bay - Kids "hang out" for little ones under 4 feet tall including shorter, wider slides. Dolphin Cove is a fun splashing, sliding, squirting, climbing adventure land for the young ones – located right next to Sandcastle Bay.

HOOSIER BAT COMPANY

4511 East Evans Avenue (SR 49 bypass exit Hwy. 2 east, left at railroad tracks)

Valparaiso 46383

❑   Phone: (800) 228-3787 **Web: www.hoosierbat.com**
❑   Admission: FREE
❑   Tours: Mornings best. Advance notice. Ages 8+. 45 minutes to one hour long. Max. 20 people.

Created by a former scout for the New York Yankees, Hoosier Bats are making an appearance on the major league scene. Hoosier Bat Company makes an all ash bat, used by many major and minor league players, and a patented three-piece wood bat, the WOODFORCE 2000. With ash in the handle, hickory in the sweet spot, and maple on the barrel end, this bat provides a solid sweet spot that will not flake, while retaining the same look and feel as a traditional all ash bat. Each year, more than 30,000 custom bats are manufactured for teams such as the White Sox, Mariners, Orioles, Indians and Brewers. Watch the patented, three-piece wood bats being made, then buy your own Hoosier Bat (or, just purchase a smaller souvenir bat in their gift shop).

PORTER COUNTY OLD JAIL MUSEUM

152 South Franklin Street

Valparaiso 46383

- ❑ Phone: (219) 465-3595
- ❑ Hours: Saturday, Sunday, Wednesday 1:00-4:00pm
- ❑ Admission: FREE

The Sheriff's home is an Italianate brick building that contains rooms of period furniture. The jail is a two-story structure leading to the Sheriff's home. See an exhibit on Wild West Bronco John (Buffalo Bill's partner) and dress from the Inaugural Ball of Abe Lincoln.

GUSE CHRISTMAS TREE FARM

6177 West 1450 South

Wanatah 46390

- ❑ Phone: (219) 733-9346
- ❑ Hours: Daily 8:00am-4:00pm (Thanksgiving-Christmas Eve)
- ❑ Admission: FREE
- ❑ Tours: By appointment. 45 minutes long. (mid-November to mid-December)

This is a 3rd and 4th generation year round business raising Christmas trees. 125 acres of trees show how different trees grow, how Christmas wreaths are made, and the operations it takes to make the finest trees. Come and cut or dig a Douglas, Fraiser Fir, Scotch, White Pine or Blue Spruce. Enjoy horse-drawn wagon rides and Santa-visits every weekend. Petting zoo and pony rides. Warm up with hot cocoa.

TIPPECANOE RIVER STATE PARK

4200 North US 35

Winamac 46996

❑   Phone: (574) 946-3213

www.in.gov/dnr/parklake/parks/tippecanoeriver.html

❑   Admission: $4.00-$5.00 per vehicle.

This park is most used for the bridle trails and excellent canoeing. During the summer when you want to swim, just take your current gate or campground receipt to Bass Lake State Beach for free admission. Warning: mosquitoes can be very annoying at times during the season. Repellent is advised! Also camping, hiking, fishing and seasonal programs (like cross-country skiing in winter).

Chapter 7
South East Area - (SE)

Our Favorites...

* Falls of the Ohio - Clarksville

* Zimmerman Art Glass - Corydon

* Squire Boone Caverns & Village - Mauckport

* Forest Discovery Center - Starlight

* State Historic Sites & State Parks

"Artists in Action"... Zimmerman Art Glass

DEAM LAKE STATE RECREATION AREA

1217 Deam Lake Road, SR 60

Borden 47106

❑   Phone: (812) 246-5421

Web: www.in.gov/dnr/forestry/forestry.html#

Deam Lake is forest property designed for recreational activities. Activities include fishing, boating, swimming, camping, picnicking, hiking, swimming, rowboat rentals, hiking trails and a Nature Center. The 194-acre lake was constructed in 1965 and was named in honor of Charles Deam, Indiana's first state forester. Deam is best known for his book, Trees of Indiana, a comprehensive study of trees throughout the state.

BROWNSTOWN SPEEDWAY

Hwy. 250, one mile southeast of town (Jackson County Fairgrounds), **Brownstown** 47220

❑   Phone: (812) 358-5332

Web: www.brownstownspeedway.com

❑   Hours: Racing Saturdays at 7:00pm (March-October).

Stock car races including Late Models, Modifieds, Street Stocks, and Bombers. Admission charged.

JACKSON-WASHINGTON STATE FOREST

1278 East SR 250 (located 2.5 miles southeast of Brownstown on St. Rd. 250), **Brownstown** 47220

❑   Phone: (812) 358-2160

Web: www.in.gov/dnr/forestry/forestry.html#

This part of the state contains unique topography known as the "knobs" region, and affords scenic views from Skyline Drive and some breathtaking hiking trails. Archery Range, Basketball and Volleyball Courts, Bridle Trails.

CHARLESTOWN STATE PARK

PO Box 38 (west of SR 62)

Charlestown 47111

❏ Phone: (812) 256-5600
   Web: www.in.gov/dnr/parklake/parks/charlestown.html
❏ Hours: Open year-round.
❏ Admission: $4.00-$5.00/vehicle.

Devonian fossils, Bird Watchers, Hiking (rugged and moderate trails available); Formerly part of the Indiana Ammunition Plant - so much of the ground is unspoiled; Camping area on site.

DERBY DINNER PLAYHOUSE

525 Marriott Drive

Clarksville 47129

❏ Phone: (812) 288-2632 or (812) 288-8281 tickets
   Web: www.derbydinner.com
❏ Hours: Performances Tuesday-Sunday. Doors open at
   6:00pm for Buffet Dinner - Show starts at 8:00pm.
   Matinees - Wednesday & Sunday. Doors open at 11:45am
   - Show at 1:30pm.
❏ Admission: Tickets: $25.00-$37.00. $14.00-$19.00 for
   Children's Breakfast or Lunch Productions. Senior
   Citizen's and Children's Discount on Friday and Sunday
   Evenings.

A dinner theater in the round featuring top-notch performances of Broadway productions served after a buffet dinner. Shows run for approximately 6 weeks and special shows are offered periodically. Children's theatre programs offered of seasonal themes or cartoon favorites (breakfast and lunch shows for these performances).

FALLS OF THE OHIO STATE PARK

201 West Riverside Drive (I – 65 Exit 0, follow signs)

Clarksville 47129

❑ Phone: (812) 280-9970, **Web: www.fallsoftheohio.org**

❑ Hours: Center open Monday-Saturday 9:00am-5:00pm, Sunday 1:00-5:00pm. Park open daily dawn to dusk. Closed Thanksgiving and Christmas

❑ Admission: $4.00 adult, $1.00 child (under age 19).

❑ Tours: Guided tours of fossil beds May-October (EDST). Classrooms November-April.

❑ Miscellaneous: Boat Launch Ramp/Ohio River, Hiking Trails, Picnicking, Bird Watching, Fishing, Gift Shop, and Ohio River and Coral Reef Aquariums.

The "Age of Fish" coral reef fossil beds are among the largest exposed Devonian fossil beds in the world. The park features a spectacular visitor center overlooking the fossil beds containing an exhibit and video presentation. While fossil collecting is prohibited, visitors are free to explore – we could identify corals, sponges, sea shells and snails. The months of August through October are the most accessible as the river is at its lowest level. Tip: It was suggested to splash water on a colony area and they will "jump out" showing exquisite detail. The Interpretive Center features a full size mammoth skeleton, plus there are exhibits on geology, history and cultural development of the Falls of the Ohio.

CORYDON CAPITOL STATE HISTORIC SITE

202 East Walnut Street (I-64 exit 105 to downtown), **Corydon 47112**

❑ Phone: (812) 738-4890
Web: www.ai.org/ism/HistoricSites/Corydon/Historic.asp

❑ Hours: Tuesday-Saturday 9:00am-5:00pm, Sunday 1:00-5:00pm. Closed Thanksgiving, Christmas Eve, Christmas Day, New Year's Day and Easter. Limited winter hours.

Corydon Capitol State Historic Site *(cont.)*

❑ Admission: FREE. Donations accepted.

❑ Miscellaneous: Guided tours, visitor center and gift shop. Several Special events are also held to celebrate Indiana's heritage.

This Site includes the restored 1816 limestone state capitol building, Governor's residence, and first state office building among other landmarks in the area. Limestone was hauled from nearby quarries to erect the 40 foot square walls, and poplar and walnut logs were cut from virgin forests from the ceiling and roof supports. In June of 1816, 43 delegates met in Corydon to draft the first state constitution. Much of their work was done under the shade of a huge elm tree. The trunk of the tree, now known as the "Constitution Elm," is still standing. The State Historic Site recounts Indiana's early days of statehood.

HARRISON CRAWFORD STATE FOREST / WYANDOTTE COMPLEX STATE FOREST

7240 Old Forest Road SW (bordering the Ohio River)

Corydon 47112

❑ Phone: (812) 738-8232.

Web: www.in.gov/dnr/forestry/forestry.html#

Timber is the key resource consideration in the management and use of Indiana's State Forests. The timber is continually evaluated to determine management needs such as harvesting, planting, thinning or timber stand improvement. Openings created by timber harvesting also increase wildlife habitat. These openings guarantee stable and healthy populations of both game and non-game species. Recreation here includes fishing, canoeing, a campground, an Olympic size swimming pool, a forestry interpretive center, several picnic areas, and hiking and horse trails.

PENNEY THE TROLLEY TOURS

341 E. Poplar (departs from Visitors Center, Walnut and Elm
streets on the northeast corner of the square)

Corydon 47112

❑   Phone: (812) 738-4846 or (888) 738-2137
Web: www.tourindiana.com/attractions.asp

❑   Admission: $5.00 adult, $2.00 child (under 12).

❑   Tours: Summer trolley rides are offered each Thursday,
Friday and Saturday at 10:30am and 1:00pm and on
Sundays at 12:30 and 2:30pm.

For the 75-minute tour, a local guide will wheel patrons
through the streets of Corydon on "Penney the Trolley". The
guide points out historic homes, businesses and other key
landmarks around Indiana's first state capital. Honk the
trolley's horn and greet townspeople who may be trimming
hedges and sweeping walks along the route. Folks wave and
call back.

ZIMMERMAN ART GLASS COMPANY

395 Valley Road (I-64 exit 105 to SR 135 South to SR 62 to
Mulberry (right turn) to Valley Road- left turn)

Corydon 47112

❑   Phone: (812) 738-2206

❑   Hours: Tuesday-Saturday 9:00am-3:00pm.

❑   Admission: FREE

❑   Tours: 30 minute demos, Tuesday-Friday only 10:00am-
1:00pm or 2:00-4:00pm.

❑   Miscellaneous: Recently produced and signed art glass
pieces available on site for purchase – you just have to
wait until they finish the piece they're working on.

Generations-old and world-renowned glass artisans make
hand-blown glass paperweights, lamps, bowls and bottles.
Two brothers work in a small workshop in an authentic

workspace so small that you can stand close to the artist. Watch as they get a glob of premixed colored molten glass and, by constantly twirling it on a long stick, begin to use old tools to shape the "glob" into their signature "flower". After a few cycles of heating/shaping/cooling the flower, they let it "twirl cool" to make the final paperweight with a blossomed flower inside. You have to see this remarkable process! Our group was speechless and mesmerized to the point that we didn't even ask questions.

SQUIRE BOONE CAVERNS AND VILLAGE

100 Squire Boone Road SW (I – 64 exit 105. Watch for signs - some pretty tricky)

Corydon (Mauckport) 47142

❑ Phone: (502) 425-CAVE or (812) 732-4382
  Web: www.squireboonecaverns.com
❑ Hours: 10:00am – 5:00pm. (Memorial Day to mid-August). Weekends only until Labor Day. Pre-scheduled the rest of the year between 10:00am – 4:00pm every two hours. Closed Thanksgiving, Christmas Eve, Christmas, New Years.
❑ Admission: $11.00 adult, $10.00 senior, $6.50 child (6-11). $3.00 parking fee per vehicle in summer. Internet coupons.
❑ Tours: Last one hour. Every 30 minutes. Group packages include hayrides and bonfires.
❑ Miscellaneous: Gem mining (fossils and gems), soap and candlemaking, petting zoo and playground (Summer only). Caverns are a constant 54 degrees year round. A light jacket is suggested.

Explore the same caverns that Squire and Daniel Boone discovered in 1790 as Squire was out searching for his older brother, Daniel who had been captured by hostile Indians. Walk past stalactites, stalagmites, blind and albino crayfish, underground streams and waterfalls, dams, and the foundation stone carved by Squire himself. It's all very quiet. Squire's life was spared when he hid in the caverns from a band of pursuing Indians – he is even buried in his beloved cave. Buy a spelunking explorer hat with light for the kids to use while they tour. Then they have a great souvenir that was actually used at the site. Onto the foundation stones of his mill, Squire Boone carved this inscription: "My God my life hath much befriended, I'll praise Him till my days are ended." Built by Squire Boone in the early 1800's, the mill area has been restored and is again grinding grain just as it did nearly two centuries ago. You can watch as the 18 foot wheel, powered by water flowing from the caverns, turns the 1,000 pound grinding stones. The miller also demonstrates how cornmeal and grits are sifted out of the ground corn. Cornmeal can be purchased at the Grist Mill.

CLARK STATE FOREST

PO Box 119 (Located on U.S. Highway 31, 10 miles south of Scottsburg or one mile north of Henryville just off I-65)

Henryville 47126

❑   Phone: (812) 294-4306
    Web: www.in.gov/dnr/forestry/forestry.html#
❑   Miscellaneous: Camping, short Hiking Trails, Seven Fishing Lakes, and Bridle Trails.

Clark State Forest, established in 1903, is the oldest state forest in Indiana. Much of this land was originally part of Clark's Grant, lands provided by a clause in the Virginia Cession of Claims to the Northwest Territory on December 20, 1783.

HOWARD STEAMBOAT MUSEUM

1101 East Market Street (I-65, exit 0)

Jeffersonville 47130

❑   Phone: (812) 283-3728 or (888) 472-0606
   Web: www.steamboatmuseum.org
❑   Hours: Tuesday-Saturday 10:00am-4:00pm, Sunday 1:00-
   4:00pm. Closed major holidays.
❑   Admission: $5.00 adult, $4.00 senior, $3.00 students (age
   6 thru college).

The museum has a large collection of steamboat models, tools, artifacts, etc. from the Great Steamboat Era. The 1894 Victorian Mansion also has many of the original furnishings and family possessions. The mansion was built by the Howard's, premier steamboat builders. Kids love seeing all the stained glass windows, especially when the sun shines through.

LAWRENCEBURG SPEEDWAY

351 East Eads Parkway (I-275 exit SR 50, Dearborn County Fairgrounds)

Lawrenceburg 47025

❑   Phone: (812) 539-4700
   Web: www.lawrenceburgspeedway.com
❑   Hours: Gates Open 5:00pm, Practice laps 6:20pm, Racing
   7:15pm. (May-September)
❑   Admission: $12.00 adult, $5.00 youth (11-15), $1.00 child
   (10 and under). Pit Passes - $20.00. Prices may vary with
   sanctioned shows/special events.

1/4 Mile High Banked Clay Oval with weekly racing divisions in Non-wing Sprints, Modifieds and Pro Stocks.

PERFECT NORTH SLOPES

19640 SR 1 (From I-275 take the US 50 Exit 16, follow ski area
signs north on Indiana Route 1)

Lawrenceburg 47025

❑ Phone: (812) 537-3754 or (513) 381-7517
   Web: www.perfectnorth.com
❑ Hours: Weekdays 9:30am-9:30pm, Weekends 9:30am-
   3:00am (December to mid-March).
❑ Admission: Flex Tickets (all day) $35.00-$40.00. Season
   Passes $100.00 and up. Children 6 & under - ski free with
   a paying adult or if taking a lesson. Active Duty Military
   & family will receive discount with valid ID.

With 70 acres of tree-lined trails and wide open slopes, they
have skiing for all abilities. They offer ski school, night
skiing, equipment rental and purchase.

CLIFTY FALLS STATE PARK

1501 Green Road (off SR 62 or 56)

Madison 47250

❑ Phone: (812) 265-4135 Inn or (812) 273-8885 park
   Web: www.in.gov/dnr/parklake/parks/cliftyfalls.html
❑ Admission: $4.00-$5.00 per vehicle.

The name Clifty Falls paints a beautiful picture in your
mind. Winter and spring hiking trails show the falls at their
best while the splendor of the creek and canyon offer
exciting scenery year-round. In historic Madison, tour the
mansion of frontier banker James F.D. Lanier and enjoy the
drive along the beautiful Ohio River. Plan a park visit during
one of the community's special events such as the Madison
Chautauqua Art Festival or Regatta hydroplane boat race.
Clifty Inn has accommodations and a Restaurant. At the Inn
is a seasonal Swimming/Pool with waterslide, tennis & other
games. Camping and a Nature Center are here too.

JEFFERSON COUNTY MUSEUM AND RAILROAD STATION DEPOT

615 West First Street (and Mill Streets on Ohio River)

Madison 47250

- ❏ Phone: (812) 265-2335, **Web: www.jcohs.org**
- ❏ Hours: Monday-Saturday 10:00am-4:30pm, Sunday 1:00-4:00pm. (May-October). Weekdays only. (November-April)
- ❏ Admission: $3.00 General.
- ❏ Miscellaneous: Octagonal Railroad Station (history of first Indiana railroad). Stop over to Dr. William Hutchings' Office (on West 3rd) or The Sullivan House (on West 2nd) for more historical county insight. Located in a historic stone house on the grounds of Madison State Hospital, the new Gatehouse Museum features photos, exhibits and artifacts telling the history of the hospital since its opening in 1910; and tracing the changes over the years in the care of mental patients. Hours: Thursday-Friday-Saturday (closed winters).

The Pioneer exhibit is a re-created stone house, typical of early rural dwellings. In it is a varied collection of early farming and domestic artifacts. The Steamboat exhibit explains the important role the Ohio River has played in the history of the area. The Civil War exhibit chronicles the famous raid of Confederate General John Hunt Morgan through the county, and explores the roles of soldiers in the Civil War. The Victorian Parlor exhibit highlights period furniture, clothing, artwork, and artifacts, all with a local history.

LANIER MANSION STATE HISTORIC SITE

511 West First Street

Madison 47250

❑ Phone: (812) 265-3526

   www.in.gov/ism/HistoricSites/LanierMansion/Historic.asp

❑ Hours: Tuesday-Saturday 9:00am-5:00pm, Sunday 1:00-
   5:00pm (mid March to mid-December). Weekends only
   (mid December to mid-March). The site is closed on
   Easter, Thanksgiving, Christmas Eve, Christmas Day and
   New Year's Day.

❑ Admission: FREE, donations accepted.

On the banks of the Ohio River stands a stately mansion
built for James Franklin Doughty Lanier - a man who, at one
time, saved Indiana from financial ruin. With national
expansion booming, Lanier's talents as a financier brought
him great fortune. The Greek Revival home is especially
noted for its staircases.

PA PAW'S FAMILY FARM

15671 Lewis Road (I-275 exit 16 (Rte. 50) west to Aurora to
Rte. 350 west)

Moores Hill 47032

❑ Phone: (812) 744-5411(farm) or (513) 821-2011
   Web: www.papawsfarm.homestead.com

❑ Hours: Spring-Fall, by reservation.

❑ Admission: $100.00 minimum per group ($5.75 per
   person). Weekday tours are 4 hours, weekend tours are 3
   hours.

❑ Miscellaneous: Bring a picnic or party - 3 spacious roofed
   shelters, a wooden red barn and small barn are available
   for learning stations and get-togethers.

Papaw's Family Farm has two main functions: Educational
and Recreational. Enjoy a tour of the farm which features a

petting zoo, palomino horses, goats and pigs. Take a walk along the creek and sit in a Native American woodland hut replica called a "waken" while you listen to stories about the Shawnee Indians and how they survived so many years ago. Learn hands-on about farming, and how to plant/harvest in the demonstration garden. A large pond (with nearby shelter) invites ecosystem study. There is a smaller spring fed woodlot pond for comparison. Minutes from the barn finds a meandering stream, a favorite for exploring students who wish to find a diversity of woodland wildlife.

CARNEGIE CENTER FOR ARTS & HISTORY/FLOYD COUNTY MUSEUM

201 East Spring Street (Eastbound on I-64, take exit #123)

New Albany 47150

❑ Phone: (812) 944-7336, **Web: www.carnegiecenter.org**
❑ Hours: Tuesday-Saturday 10:00am-5:30pm
❑ Admission: FREE, donations accepted.

The contemporary art gallery and local history museum has permanent and temporary traveling exhibits. This is the home of the famous "Yenowine Folk Art Dioramas - a hand-carved animated diorama depicting scenes from early Indiana.

CULBERTSON MANSION STATE HISTORIC PARK

914 East Main Street (off I-64), **New Albany** 47150

❑ Phone: (812) 244-9600
   www.ai.org/ism/HistoricSites/Culbertson/Historic.asp
❑ Hours: Tuesday-Saturday 9:00am-5:00pm, Sunday 1:00-5:00pm. Closed on Mondays, Thanksgiving, Christmas Eve, Christmas Day, New Year's Day and Easter. Closed mid-December to mid-March.

❑   Admission: FREE, donations accepted.

A Victorian mansion that stands as an impressive tribute to one of Indiana's leading merchants and philanthropists, William Culbertson. The Culbertson Mansion represents the lifestyles of the Victorian fortune-makers as well as the lifestyles of the servant staffs. Visitors may view the grand parlors, dining rooms, bedrooms, kitchen and laundry room of the 25 room mansion.

OHIO COUNTY HISTORICAL MUSEUM

212 South Walnut Street

Rising Sun 47040

❑   Phone: (812) 438-4915
   Web: www.ohiocountyinmuseum.org
❑   Hours: Daily, except Wednesday 11:00am-4:00pm.
   Sunday 1:30-4:30pm.
❑   Admission: $1.00-$2.50 (age 13+), FREE child (under 12).

Home of "Hoosier Boy" a 1900 racing boat with the fastest time between Louisville and Cincinnati. On October 5, 2003, the "Hoosier Girl", the sister boat to the Hoosier Boy, came home. The Hoosier Girl was built in the 1940s after the first one (built 1908) sunk in the early 1940s. She is an exact duplicate of the original boat. The museum has an original Auto Harp - first coin operated music player.

HARDY LAKE STATE RESERVOIR

4171 East Harrod Road

Scottsburg 47170

❑   Phone: (812) 794-3800.
   Web: www.in.gov/dnr/parklake/reservoirs/hardy.html

2,178 acres and a 741-acre lake provide facilities like: Archery Range, Sport Courts, Horseshoe Pits, Boating,

Camping, Cultural Arts Programs, Fishing / Ice Fishing, Hiking Trails, Interpretive / Recreational Programs, Picnicking / Shelter houses, Playgrounds, Rental-Rowboat, Swimming / Beach, and Water-skiing.

PIGEON ROOST STATE HISTORIC SITE

(5 miles south of Scottsburg on US 31)

Scottsburg 47170

❑ Phone: (812) 265-3526
www.in.gov/ism/HistoricSites/PigeonRoost/Historic.asp
❑ Hours: Open dawn to dusk.
❑ Admission: FREE, donations accepted.

The first of several conflicts in the Indiana Territory during the War of 1812 occurred at the small settlement of Pigeon Roost in Scott County—a few miles south of present-day Scottsburg. The site is a 44 foot limestone monument memorializing 24 settlers killed during an 1812 raid. The immediate result of the Pigeon Roost conflict was the effect it had on settlers. Fearing further attacks, communities surrounding Pigeon Roost moved into forts and blockhouses. Settlers planned more militia raids on Native American settlements across the Indiana Territory. Skirmishes between settlers and tribes continued until the Treaty of Ghent was signed in 1814 ending the War of 1812.

FOREST DISCOVERY CENTER

533 Louis Smith Road (I – 64 exit 119. Follow signs for Hubers)

Starlight 47106

❑ Phone: (812) 923-1590, **Web: www.forestcenter.com**
❑ Hours: Tuesday-Saturday 9:00am-5:00pm.
❑ Admission: $5.50 adult, $4.50 senior (55+), $3.00 child (6 –12)
❑ Tours: Manufacturing Tour: (Eastern time) Tuesday – Friday. 9:00am-1:30pm. Every ½ hour.

❑ Miscellaneous: Gift shop with wood artwork, toys, souvenirs.

As you enter from the lobby you'll explore the unique indoor forest made from wood products, complete with forest sounds (birds, brush). It's hard to tell it isn't really indoor forest trees! Before heading upstairs, view the short orientation film narrated by Oakie Acorn. Once upstairs, you can walk through an enormous giant oak tree where you can view videos and sign the tree in support of re-forestation efforts. Next, gaze at the 1000 sq. ft. mural created from small wood inlays using age-old techniques called "marquetry". Artisans are usually available to show you how it was done. A glass enclosed skywalk brings you to a real, working company rough mill. Arrows and signs describe how logs become trimmed and molded. They don't waste anything…even the sawdust left over is burned as fuel for the electric generators. Defective wood chunks are made into mulch. The 13 step process begins with sawed logs, then dried in kilns to remove moisture, then planed, then electronically cut and finally jointed or sorted by size of "clear" (non-defective) board.

STARVE HOLLOW STATE RECREATION AREA

4345 South CR 275 West, **Vallonia** 47281

❑ Phone: (812) 358-3464.

Web: www.in.gov/dnr/forestry/forestry.html#

When it was first constructed in 1938, Starve Hollow Lake was the largest body of water, in wide area, in Indiana. The lake now covers 145 acres. Although no longer Indiana's largest lake, Starve Hollow Lake offers some of the best fishing in southern Indiana. Volleyball, Softball & Basketball, Camping and Swimming, too.

VERSAILLES STATE PARK

Box 205, US 50

Versailles 47042

❑   Phone: (812) 689-6424

Web: www.in.gov/dnr/parklake/parks/versailles.html

❑   Admission: $4.00-$5.00 per vehicle.

Relax while fishing on the 230-acre lake where you can rent a paddleboat, rowboat or canoe. Bring your bicycle and pedal the nearby 27-mile Hoosier Hills Bicycle Route. Also Bridle Trails, Swimming / Pool and waterslide.

SUGGESTED LODGING AND DINING

SCHIMPFF'S CONFECTIONERY - **Jeffersonville**. 347 Spring Street. **www.schimpffs.com**. Phone: (812) 283-8367. Famous for their cinnamon red hots. Schimpff's is a fourth generation, family-owned business that features a soda fountain, original tin ceiling, antique memorabilia and tasty candies.

MUNDT'S CANDIES / JWI CONFECTIONARY - **Madison**. (I-65, Ohio River Scenic Route). Phone: (812) 265-6171 or **www.mundtscandies.com**. Hours: Tuesday - Saturday 11:00am - 5:00pm, Sunday Noon-4:00pm. Open weekend evenings seasonally. This historic candy store and soda fountain serves gourmet desserts/ lunches throughout the day. "Lunch at Mundt's" is the place where the famous "fish" candy is made.

Chapter 8
South West Area - (SW)

Our Favorites...

* Angel Mounds Historic Site - Evansville

* Evansville Museum of Arts, History, and Science - Evansville

* Log Inn - Haubstadt

* Turner Doll Factory - Heltonville

* Lincoln Boyhood Home Attraction - Lincoln City

* Grouseland - Vincennes

* Indiana Territory Capitol Village - Vincennes

Angel Mounds Prehistoric Indian Dwelling

BLUESPRING CAVERNS PARK

1459 Bluespring Caverns Road (US 50 and SR 37 on CR 450 South)

Bedford 47421

❑ Phone: (812) 279-9471

Web: www.bluespringcaverns.com

❑ Hours: Daily 9:00am-5:00pm. (May-October), Weekends only (April, May) EST.

❑ Admission: $12.00 adult, $6.00 child (3-15). The tour is not recommended for infants and very young children. The walk into the Caverns to our tour boats and back to the surface is 800 feet and is a fairly steep ramp.

❑ Tours: Tours hourly or more often on Saturdays & Sundays and during the summer.

❑ Miscellaneous: Always a 52 degree constant temperature – a light jacket recommended. Myst'ry River Gemstone Mine – prospect for your own gemstones. "Overnight Adventures" for organized youth groups.

Years ago the White River cut into small cracks in limestone rock and dissolved it forming cave passages. As glaciers moved into the area they brought debris of soil and rock that were deposited. In the 1940's, a large pond on a farm disappeared overnight to reveal the entrance to the cave. The Myst'ry River tour boat glides along the quiet waters into the heart of a subterranean natural world. The guide will point out unusual formations and the interesting albino blind fish and crawfish that live in darkness.

HOOSIER STATE FOREST

811 Constitution Avenue (Brownstown Ranger District)

Bedford 47421

❑   Phone: (812) 275-5987 (Brownstown) and (812) 547-7051 (Tell City Ranger), **Web: www.fs.fed.us/r9/hoosier**

Situated in the rolling hills of south central Indiana, the Hoosier hides its geologic landscapes beneath a canopy of hickory and oak. A little exploration reveals a landscape of underground rivers, caves, sinkholes, box canyons, limestone bluffs, and narrow ridges. The most popular spots are:

❑   <u>WATCHABLE WILDLIFE SITES</u> - Buzzard Roost Overlook is located approximately two miles north of Magnet.

❑   <u>CHARLES C. DEAM WILDERNESS</u> - Indiana's only Congressionally designated wilderness area has 13,000 acres providing for solitude and a remote experience.

❑   <u>HICKORY RIDGE LOOKOUT TOWER</u> - Constructed by the CCC in 1939.

❑   <u>PIONEER MOTHERS MEMORIAL FOREST</u> - An 88 acre virgin old-growth forest and archaeological site. Explore virgin forest of ancient oaks and 130-foot walnut trees with 42-inch diameters.

❑   <u>LICK CREEK SETTLEMENT</u> - site of a 1815-1900 African American settlement.

❑   <u>HEMLOCK CLIFFS</u> - a box-shaped canyon with sandstone formations, seasonal water falls and rock shelters. And, of course, the canyon's cool climate is perfect for hemlock -- these tall evergreens with short needles and small cones simply thrive in this environment and so will you. Hemlock Cliffs is located west of Highway 37 about two miles north of Interstate 64.

❑ RICKENBAUGH HOUSE - A stone house built in 1874, used as a local post office and church meeting house.

❑ SUNDANCE LAKE - a 5 acre lake named for a Native American spiritual dance held annually near the site.

❑ CLOVER LICK BARRENS - Shallow soils and rock outcrops are found in these prairie-like, fire-dependant ecosystems which have many rare species.

❑ WESLEY CHAPEL GULF - This National Natural Landmark is an 8 acre collapsed sinkhole with a floor which provides a window to the underground river system.

❑ BUFFALO TRACE - an historic pathway used by migrating buffalo from the Falls of the Ohio River near Louisville to Vincennes where they crossed into the Illinois prairie.

❑ TIPSHAW LAKE BEACH - This beach offers a combination of sand and sun, or shady grass-covered hillside.

The Ohio River and the forest's four lakes offer a little something for everyone, including swimming, waterfowl viewing, canoeing, boating, and fishing for catfish and bass.

TURNER DOLL FACTORY
RR 1, Heltonville - Bartlettsville Road (Highway 50, best to call for directions or from website). East to 446 North to Highway 58 [Left], [Right, off 58 at school], Follow signs)

Bedford (Heltonville) 47436

❑ Phone: (812) 834-6692; (800) 887-6372
   Web: www.turnerdolls.com

❑ Hours: Monday-Friday 10:00am-5:00pm, Saturday 10:00am-4:00pm.

❑ Admission: FREE

❑ Tours: Monday-Friday 9:00am-3:00 pm. Best to call ahead to be sure they are in production.

Turner Doll Factory *(cont.)*

❏   Miscellaneous: Gift Shop with over-run discounted dolls. Located on farm property so the non-doll lovers can wander outside to see the variety of animals. They will send you a map to the exact location of property.

How are dolls' eyes popped in? This, and many questions you wouldn't even think to ask are answered during this delightfully explained tour. The vinyl parts of a doll are made with liquid that looks like thick, light chocolate milk. Liquid vinyl is poured into the mold of a head, arm or leg and then put in a rotating oven. How do they get the vinyl to coat just the outside of the mold and not fill the inside? Artists hand-paint the faces and add accents of blush (with an airbrush) to certain parts of the arms and legs to make them look real. Next, the doll is assembled and stuffed with "fluff" and beads in just the right places so when you hold the baby doll, it feels real! Each doll has its own name and outfit (hand-sewn by locals). Our favorite is the "Kradle Kids" collection - they have such cute "pouty faces".

PATOKA LAKE STATE RESERVOIR
RR 1, **Birdseye** 47513

❏   Phone: (812) 685-2464 or (812) 547-7028
    Web: www.explore-si.com/PatokaLake.html

Archery range, Frisbee Golf Course, Solar Heated Visitors Center (illustrated displays on wildlife, history, birds of prey, solar energy and the viewing of a live bald eagle are all part of the Center's Raptor Education Program), house-boating, water-skiing, swimming, and fishing. Large campgrounds, launching ramps, marina, paved biking trails and a large supervised beach and swimming (Memorial to Labor Day). Lodging is available at cozy cabins and rustic chalets near or on the lake.

PERRY COUNTY MUSEUM

PO Box 36 (Seventh & Taylor Streets, old County Courthouse)

Cannelton 47520

❑   Phone: (812) 547-3190

www.perrycountyindiana.org/attract/pccourthouse.html

❑   Hours: Sunday 1:00-4:00pm and by appointment.

Early Perry County life is set in displays of the following: Coal- Clay - Cotton Textile Industries, Native American Artifacts, Civil War and Other War Memorabilia, Perry County Fossils and Minerals, Blacksmith Shop - Carpenter's Shop - Stone Mason's exhibit, "The Victorian Parlor" of 1870, and a media center on military, river history and steamboats.

DR. TED'S MUSICAL MARVELS

11896 South US 231 (I-64 exit 57 to US 231 North)

Dale 47523

❑   Phone: (812) 937-4250

Web: www.drteds.com/museum.html

❑   Hours: Monday-Saturday 10:00am-6:00pm, Sunday 1:00-6:00pm (Memorial Day-Labor Day). Weekends only in May & September.

❑   Admission: $2.00-$5.00 (age 6+).

❑   Miscellaneous: Gift shop

Take a guided tour (90 minutes) of wonderful collection of restored mechanical musical instruments including music boxes, street organs, nickelodeons. Takes you back in time to the hey day of amusement parks and carousels. Actually hear them played. You won't be listening to taped music...each manual music maker actually "plays" music of a century ago. They crash their own cymbals, play their own pipes, beat their own drums, all produced by cranking, and forcing air through holes that move pulleys and bellows that operate the instrument. Something amazing is going on inside the machine to play the right note at the right time. Bring the grandparents along, for sure, on this trip.

GRAHAM FARMS CHEESE

State Route 57 North

Elnora 47529

❑ Phone: (812) 692-5237 or (800) 472-9178
   Web: www.grahamcheese.com
❑ Hours: Monday-Saturday 8:00am-6:00pm, Sunday Noon-5:00pm.
❑ Admission: FREE
❑ Tours: Best times for a tour are Monday, Wednesday, and Friday before 11:00am. These are the days they are making cheese. They will do tours on Tuesday and Thursday, but will consist of seeing the machinery only. Tours last approximately 15 minutes. They do have a ten minute video playing in the store in case you miss the tour.

View cheesemaking (they've been making it since 1928). Cheese sampling. Ask how early Amish farmers brought their raw milk in the morning. Purdue and State of Indiana cheeses are a must souvenir.

WESSELMAN WOODS NATURE PRESERVE

551 North Boeke Road (I-164 to SR 66)

Evansville 47711

❑ Phone: (812) 479-0771
   Web: www.wesselman.evansville.net/index.htm
❑ Hours: Trails, 7:00am-7:00pm (April-September), 8:00am-4:00pm (October-March). Nature Center - 9:00am-5:00pm (April-September), 8:00am-4:00pm (October-March). Closed Mondays & Thanksgivingtime, Xmastime, New Years time.

❑ Admission: FREE. Other than during special events, there is no fee to enter the preserve or nature center although donations are accepted.

An ancient forest with 200 acres of bottomland hardwood forest, fields and ponds. The Nature Center has trail maps, lists of wildflowers, birds and trees to look for and brochures covering maple sugaring, pioneer skills and forestry. The preserve - where you can also find a section of the historic Wabash & Erie Canal - is home to myriad wildflowers, deer, birds, and a host of other wildlife. Stop by the Nature Center and leaf through exhibits and a wildlife observation room.

EVANSVILLE MUSEUM OF ARTS, HISTORY AND SCIENCE

411 SE Riverside Drive (downtown in Sunset Park, at the corner of Cherry St and Riverside Dr. (Veterans Memorial Parkway becomes Riverside Drive one block from the Museum)

Evansville 47713

❑ Phone: (812) 425-2406, **Web: www.emuseum.org**

❑ Hours: Tuesday-Saturday 10:00am-5:00pm. Sunday Noon-5:00pm. CDT. Closed on New Year's Day, Memorial Day, Easter Sunday, Independence Day, Labor Day, Thanksgiving, Christmas Eve and Christmas Day.

❑ Admission: $2.00 adult, $1.00 child. EMTRAC admission $2.00 adult. Children under 12 are free if accompanied by an adult. Admission to Koch Planetarium $3.00 adult, $2.00 child (3-12).

❑ Miscellaneous: Museum Shop. Collection of artwork from the 16th century to the present and an Anthropology gallery on the two upper levels. Koch Planetarium has "themed" programs weekly.

Explore prehistoric, Native American and Main Street (late 1800's) History. Old-style tools they used, types of buildings they lived in, and what the kids played with back then. What was it like to live in a river city at the turn of the 20th Century? Take a walk through Rivertown, USA for an historic look at early Evansville. Using the ceramic sculpture, The Kingdom Builders, students compare similarities in the early cultures of Egypt and Mexico. The Science Center for school-aged and pre-school kids has hands-on exhibits dealing with lasers, optical illusions, gravity and spatial relationships - all very applicable to everyday situations. Many "theme" exhibits focus on subjects like weather or the "art of science". The Transportation Center (outside) – "EMTRAC" focuses on modes of early transport - dugout canals, steam boats, autos, and steam locomotives.

ANGEL MOUNDS STATE HISTORIC SITE

8215 Pollack Avenue (I -164 to Highway 662, Covert Avenue Exit)

Evansville 47715

- ❑   Phone: (812) 853-3956, **Web: www.angelmounds.org**
- ❑   Hours: Tuesday-Saturday 9:00am-5:00pm, Sunday and Holidays, 1:00-5:00pm (mid-March to mid-December)
- ❑   Admission: Donations. Most special events require admission by ticket or parking fee.
- ❑   Miscellaneous: Interpretive Center. Nature preserve. Picnic Area.

Located on the banks of the Ohio River, this is a well-preserved prehistoric Indian settlement of the Mississippians who planted corn, hunted and fished for food in the area for over 250 years. The Indians had 1000 - 3000 people populate the area. 11 earthen mounds served as elevated buildings until mysteriously abandoned. The site also includes reconstructed winter houses, a round house, summer houses, a stockade and a temple that formed a village within the mounds. Learn about home and fortress construction - do you know what "waffle" and "daub" mean? -- (twigs woven between logs, then plastered with clay). The Middle-Mississippi tribe were known for their pottery and animal-shaped toys made from clay with added crushed mussel shells (used as a tempering agent). A popular kids game called "chunky" is played by throwing spears at small rolling stone discs. The closest spear wins. The earthen, thatched living huts had heating and air-conditioning - how?

HANDS ON DISCOVERY CHILDREN'S MUSEUM
Evansville 47715

❏   Phone: (812) 477-4929
     Web: www.handsondiscovery.org
❏   Hours: New hours will be posted on our website updates pages.

NOTE: A new children's museum for Evansville and the Tri-State is anticipated to open in late 2006 in the historic former Central Library building in downtown Evansville. The old location (Washington Square Mall) is closed in preparation for the move. The new museum will include interactive exhibits designed to support academic learning goals of area schools as well as the interests of area and visiting children.

A place for kids ages 3-12 and their adults where children "play to learn" and adults "learn to play". Learn about health and nutrition with Stuffee; pretend you're on a TV news set; see Seascape ocean creatures; pretend to have a meal at the International Diner; play music or perform; Touch the Future in the NASA galaxy; importance of thumbs and healthy teeth; computer and the arts; or finish in the Rain Forest or Fantasy Forest play areas (how about all that rice?).

MESKER PARK ZOO AND BOTANIC GARDEN

2421 Bement Avenue (off SR 66, Mesker Park)

Evansville 47720

❏ Phone: (812) 428-0715, **Web: www.meskerparkzoo.com**
❏ Hours: Daily 9:00am-5:00pm.
❏ Admission: $3.00-$4.00 (ages 3+). $2.00-$3.00 extra per transport activity or animal feed.

The rolling hills of this 70 some acres are home to approximately 600 animals. Indiana's largest zoo includes a petting zoo, zoo train, Lake Victoria paddle boat rides, Discovery Center rain forest and Jungle Cafe. Resident monkeys live in the center of a lake in a concrete replica of Christopher Columbus' Santa Maria. The zoo is divided into the African Panorama, Tropical Americas, Asian Valley, Lemur Forest, and North America forest - including lions and a tiger, birds of all feathers, monkeys and lemurs, gazelle and giraffe, kangaroos and kudus, leopards and a warthog, zebras & zebus.

PIKE STATE FOREST

6583 East SR 364 (off State Road 364, four miles east of State Road 61)

Ferdinand 47532

❏ Phone: (812) 367-1524
Web: www.state.in.us/dnr/forestry/stateforests/pike.htm

Topography at Pike State Forest varies from hilly uplands to the low bottomlands of the Patoka River. Because of the diversity of sites, a wide variety of plant and animal life make their homes at Pike. Several recreational opportunities are available at Pike State Forest, including hunting, horseback riding, picnicking, bird watching and hiking.

FRENCH LICK SPRINGS RESORT

8670 West State Road 56

French Lick 47432

❑   Phone: (800) 457-4042 reservations or (812) 936-9300
    Web: www.frenchlick.com

Reasonable resort accommodations with kid-friendly activities like: Archery, Badminton, Basketball, Bike Rental, Bingo, Board Games, Boating (Patoka Lake), Bowling, Croquet, Fishing (Patoka Lake), Golf, Horseback Riding, Miniature Golf, Playground, Kids Club with childcare and planned activities, Playground, Nature Hikes, Pony Rides, Rec Center (arcade), Skiing (Paoli Peaks), Surrey Rides, Swimming (indoor/outdoor), Tennis (indoor /outdoor), Train Rides (IN Railway Museum), Trolley Rides and Volleyball. Some activities are available during season (May - October) only. Availability of some activities is subject to weather conditions. Many activities charge separate fees. Parents can play golf or go to the spa springs treatments while kids are at the Kids Club.

INDIANA RAILWAY MUSEUM AND TRAIN RIDES

SR 56, 1 Monon Street (SR 37 to Paoli, go West on Hwy 56/150 to French Lick), **French Lick** 47432

❑   Phone: (812) 936-2405 or (800) 74-TRAIN
    Web: www.indianarailwaymuseum.org
❑   Hours: Weekends and Holidays 10:00am, 1:00pm & 4:00 pm. (April-October)
❑   Admission: $9.00 adult, $5.00 child (3-11)
❑   Tours: 2 hour, 20 mile train trip.
❑   Miscellaneous: Train Robbery Rides one weekend per month including Memorial Day, July 4th and Labor Day weekends. Gift Shop and snacks.

Indiana Railway Museum And Train Rides *(cont.)*

The museum displays diesel and steam locomotives, a rare railway Post Office car and a 1951 dining car. The Springs Valley Electric Trolley (shortest trolley line in the world) carries passengers for a little ride for a little fee ($1.00-2.00). Take the Train Ride through 20 miles of Hoosier National Forest and the 2200 ft. Burton Tunnel (one of the longest railroad tunnels in the state). The area's history is related by uniformed crew members - many who have personal stories to tell.

COLONEL WILLIAM JONES STATE HISTORIC SITE

Rte. 1, Box 600 (one mile west of US 231 on Boone Street)

Gentryville 47537

❑ Phone: (812) 937-2802
   www.state.in.us/ism/HistoricSites/Jones/Historic.asp
❑ Hours: Wednesday-Saturday 9:00am-5:00pm, Sunday 1:00-5:00pm (mid-March to mid-December). Closed on Thanksgiving, Christmastime, New Year's and Easter.
❑ Admission: FREE. Donations accepted.
❑ Miscellaneous: Situated on 100 acres of forest, the property also offers a self-guiding nature trail, picnic area and a restored log barn.

This carefully restored 1834 Federal-design home of the merchant employer of Abraham Lincoln offers a unique look at the early development of Indiana and the life of Colonel William Jones, who was also a politician, farmer and soldier. The home includes guided tours, themed talks, and exhibits.

LOG INN

Old State Rd (RR 2, I-64 to US 41 East), **Haubstadt** 47639

❑ Phone: (812) 867-3216
❑ Hours: Tuesday-Thursday 4:00-9:00pm, Friday-Saturday
 4:00-10:00pm.
❑ Admission: Around $10.00 adult, $5.00 child for Family
 Style Dinners.

Built in 1825 as a Noon Day Stage Coach Stop and Trading Post. Dine in the same original Log Room that Abraham Lincoln stopped at in November, 1844, enroute back from visiting his mother's grave. It was part of his campaign speaking tour. Officially recognized as the oldest restaurant in Indiana, authentic 1-foot thick logs surround you as you eat their wonderful fried chicken meals. Take time to read the articles on the walls while you wait for dinner. Dinners served by a la carte menu or family style.

DUBOIS COUNTY MUSEUM

1103 Main Street (Gramelspacher-Gutzweiler Bldg.)

Jasper 47546

❑ Phone: (812) 634-7733 or (800) 968-4578
 Web: www.duboiscounty.org/Museum.htm
❑ Hours: Friday and Saturday 10:00am-2:00pm. EST
❑ Admission: FREE. Donations accepted.

The Museum traces the region's dynamic history from the Ice Age to the present. Archaic Indians roamed the forests and glens that once blanketed this land. They were followed by the Piankshaw Indians, who preceded the Scots-Irish settlers. An overwhelming migration of Germans arrived in the Mid-Nineteenth Century. Visit a log cabin home of early settlers, stop by the Mercantile for some fashion tips, and also discover the death rituals of the early people.

INDIANA BASEBALL HALL OF FAME

1436 Leopold Street, Hwy. 162 & College Avenue (Campus of Vincennes Univ. - Jasper, Ruxer Student Center)

Jasper 47546

❑ Phone: (812) 482-2262
   Web: www.indbaseballhalloffame.org
❑ Hours: 9:00am-5:00pm during the school year from August - June, during summer, and on weekends (11:00am-3:00pm) Closed legal holidays.

The sponsoring body of the hall of fame is the Indiana High School Baseball Coaches Association, IHSBCA, which has served the baseball coaches of Indiana since 1971. The first inductions were in July 1979 and there are currently 91 inductees in the hall of fame in four categories: pro-player, coach-manager (high school, college, pro), contributor and veteran.

WYANDOTTE CAVES

(I – 64 to SR 66 South to SR 62 East)

Leavenworth 47137

❑ Phone: (812) 738-2782, **Web: www.cccn.net**
❑ Hours: Daily 9:00am-5:00pm. (Spring -Summer-Fall). EDST.
❑ Admission:$12.00-16.00 adult, $6.00-8.00 child. Combo pricing available as well as, Natural Explorers youth program pricing.
❑ Miscellaneous: Children 12 and under must be with an adult. Caves are a constant 52 degrees.

Reservations must be made for a guided 3, 5 or 7 hour tour. These tours offer serious spelunkers a real challenge with several long crawls and some climbing. Lights and helmets are provided, as are lockers and shower facilities. SIBERTS

CAVE - FLOWSTONE FALLS TOUR – short and easy with flowstone and dripstone formations. Indirect electrical lighting. 1/2 mile, 30-45 minute tour. March-October. WYANDOTTE CAVE - MONUMENT MOUNTAIN TOUR – deep cave with formations like helictites, gypsum/flint quarries. Learn the history and geology of Wyandotte Cave as you take an expedition through its vast halls and over its rugged terrain. On this tour, you will see what is considered to be one of the world's largest underground mountains. 1 ½ miles of steep terrain and stairs in lighted passageways. 90 minutes. May- Labor Day.

BUFFALO RUN GRILL & GIFTS
Highway 162 (one mile from Lincoln Boyhood National Memorial, just south of I-64)

Lincoln City 47552

❑   Phone: (812) 937-2799
     Web: www.legendaryplaces.org/buffalorun/default.htm
❑   Hours: Daily, except Tuesday 11:00am-7:00pm CDT
     (Memorial Day-Labor Day). Saturday/Sunday 10:00am-
     7:00pm CST (Labor Day to mid-December).
❑   Tours: Please call for prices and arrangements.

Buffalo Run Grill & Gifts offers buffalo and ostrich burgers which are lower in fat than turkey. Live buffalo and ostrich can be seen grazing behind the business. Experience the sights of true pioneer living with buffalo roaming behind a frontier encampment (during special seasonal events). Frontier crafts, demonstrations and trading goods are available along with bison products in the gift shop. Farm tours are also available with pre-tour reservation or during special events. Expect to enter the teepee with a Native American, join a pioneer in the Legendary Lincoln Cabin, view and feed the buffalo herd, and enjoy a fun and educational visit.

LINCOLN BOYHOOD NATIONAL MEMORIAL

SR 162 (I-64 exit 57, US 231 south thru Dale to Gentryville.
Then, east on SR 162 for 2 miles), **Lincoln City** 47552

- ❑   Phone: (812) 937-4541, **Web: www.nps.gov/libo/**
- ❑   Hours: Open From December-February 8:00am-4:30pm.
      Open From March through November 8:00am-5:00pm.
      The farm is staffed from mid-April through September.
      CDT.
- ❑   Admission: Admission to the park is $3.00 per person for
      age 17 and older, with a maximum charge of $5.00/family.
- ❑   Miscellaneous: Picnic Shelter.

The Visitor Center is a museum with film "Here I Grew Up" (from age 7-21 years) - young Abe Lincoln. The Cabin site is a working pioneer farmstead with animals and crops where Abraham used to split rails, plant and plow or milk cows. See his mother's grave (she died of "milksick" when he was 9 years old). We learned that "milksick" is a disease caused by poisonous milk produced by cows that eat snakeroot (if pastures are dry, cows migrate to forest areas where poisonous plants grow). Walk on the Boyhood Nature Trails - the same trails that a young Abraham would have walked alone in thought years ago.

YOUNG ABE LINCOLN MUSICAL DRAMA/ LINCOLN STATE PARK

Lincoln State Park Amphitheatre (I-64, Exit 57 to US 231 South)

Lincoln City 47552

- ❑   Phone: (812) 937-4710 (park) or (800) 264-4223
      Web: www.lincoln-amphitheatre.com
- ❑   Hours: Wednesday-Sunday, 7:30 pm CDT . Reservations
      best. (mid-June to mid-August). See website for schedule
      of which play is showing each night. They show one other
      drama each summer on alternate days.

- ❑ Admission: $17.00 adult, $15.00 senior (60+), $8.00 child (under 18).
- ❑ Tours: Backstage $2.00/person before shows.
- ❑ Miscellaneous: Sunday Family Night and Kid's Day Special Pricing. Completely covered amphitheatre. No rain checks.

See the Story of Lincoln's Youth in Southern Indiana. Relive the early 1800's on the Indiana frontier as over 40 actors become (very believable) Lincoln family and friends. See him deal with the death of his mother and sister and his first brush with slavery. Experience the touching, funny and serious sides of youth that developed him into a well respected man. Lincoln State Park is a scenic 1,747-acre park established in 1932 as a memorial to Nancy Hanks Lincoln. Recreational facilities include Lake Lincoln, lakeside shelter house, boat rental building, nature center, cabins, picnic areas, shelters and trails, plus Class A and primitive camp sites.

CAVE COUNTRY CANOES - BLUE RIVER

PO Box 217, 112 Main Street

Marengo 47140

- ❑ Phone: (812) 365-2705
  Web: www.cavecountrycanoes.com
- ❑ Season: (April-October)
- ❑ Admission: $18.00-$22.00 per person.
- ❑ Tours: Half day (2-4 hours) and Full day (4-7 hours) trips, guided. All rates include paddle, lifejacket, map and transportation.

Two bases to serve you... Milltown & Leavenworth. Enjoy canoes, kayaks & shuttle service on the Blue River ... the most spring fed of all Indiana's streams. The many springs account for the aqua-blue color of the river, leading to the name "The Blue". In many areas limestone bluffs, dotted with cave entrances, tower above the river attesting to the fact that "The Blue" flows through the heart of Indiana's Cave Country. The river valley is noted for its abundant wildlife, natural beauty, and excellent fishing.

MARENGO CAVE
400 East State Road 64 (I – 64 to SR 66 and SR 64 west)
Marengo 47140

❑   Phone: (812) 365-2705, **Web: www.marengocave.com**
❑   Hours: Daily 9:00 am-6:00 pm. (Summer). 9:30am-
5:30pm (Spring and Fall). 9:00am-5:00 pm (Winter).
Closed Christmas and Thanksgiving Day. EST.
❑   Admission: $12.00-$13.00 adult, Half-price fee child (4–
12). Combine tours and save $3.00-$6.00 per person.
❑   Tours: Leave every 30 minutes
❑   Miscellaneous: Hungry Grotto Snack Shop. Cave Springs
Mining Company – gemstone mining – Daily, (April-
October). Climbing Tower. Canoe trips, trail rides. Camping.

Tours include:

❑   <u>CRYSTAL PALACE TOUR</u> – 40 minutes, world famous
"Crystal Palace" cave room with dramatic lighting
presentation. Mountain rooms and massive deposits.
❑   <u>DRIPSTONE TRAIL TOUR</u> – One hour and 10 minutes.
Known for soda straw formations, slender and intricate
"dripping" deposits. Includes "Pulpit Rock", "Music Hall"
and "Penny Ceiling".
❑   <u>THE CRAWL</u> – challenging, simulated cave maze crawl.
Do you have what it takes to be a cave explorer? Physically
fit ages 8–30 only. Claustrophobia City! Best to try before
the Cave Exploring trip is purchased. $2.00.

❑ <u>CAVE EXPLORING TRIPS</u> – age 10 and up. Don a lighted helmet and old clothes and crawl through undeveloped new cave passages. Be sure to get a picture of yourself on this excursion. Friends won't believe it!

SPRING MILL STATE PARK

PO Box 376 (SR 37 to SR 60 East), **Mitchell** 47446

❑ Phone: (812) 849-4129
    Web: www.in.gov/dnr/parklake/parks/springmill.html
❑ Admission: $4.00-$5.00 per vehicle.

Lots to do and see here…Beginning with the Spring Mill Inn (812) 849-4081 - Accommodations and Restaurant. Tour the restored Pioneer Village including a gristmill, lime kiln, sawmill, hat shop, post office, apothecary and boot shop. Plan to take a boat ride into Twin Caves (tour times are assigned daily, they are seasonal) or walk into Donaldson cave. Grissom Memorial honors Hoosier astronaut "Gus" Grissom, one of seven Mercury astronauts and America's second man in space (space capsule and video of space exploration). Other facilities include: Indoor Swimming/Pool, Tennis & other games, Camping, Cultural Arts Programs, Fishing / Ice Fishing, Hiking Trails, Nature Center / Interpretive Services, and a Saddle Barn.

GASTOF AMISH VILLAGE

City Road 650 East (off US 150)

Montgomery 47558

❑ Phone: (812) 486-3977 or (812) 486–2600
    Web: www.gastofamishvillage.com
❑ Hours: Monday-Saturday. Lunch/Dinner. Breakfast Tuesday, Wednesday, & Saturday only.

Tours by buggy pass a harness shop, quilt and craft shop, general store and candy factory. The restaurant, built of

Indiana oak and poplar, was framed by Amish carpenters with simple joints and pegs. Amish cooking. Many "Amish" or "Harvest" Festivals are held at site year-round.

HARMONIE STATE PARK

3451 Harmonie State Park Road (Off CR 69 - on the banks
of the Wabash)

New Harmony 47631

❑ Phone: (812) 682-4821.
Web: www.in.gov/dnr/parklake/parks/harmonie.html
❑ Admission: $4.00-$5.00 per vehicle.

Located "on the banks of the Wabash," 25 miles northwest of Evansville, this park has a beautiful swimming pool, shady picnic areas, and ravines. Trails for walking, biking and nature hikes will lure you for a visit. They also have cabins and a Nature Center.

PAOLI PEAKS SKI & SNOWBOARD RESORT

2798 W. CR 25 S

Paoli 47454

❑ Phone: (812) 723-4696, **Web: www.paolipeaks.com**
❑ Hours: Monday-Thursday 10:00am-9:30pm, Friday 10:00am-10:00pm and Friday & Saturday Midnight-6:00am, Saturday 9:00am-10:00pm, Sunday 9:00am-9:30pm. See website for special holiday hours.
❑ Admission: Every activity involves a fee. Many packages available. Go online for best information.

On the Slopes there is a natural hill with 300 ft. vertical drop. Average grade: 10%-15%. Terrain: 25% beginner, 55% intermediate, 10% advanced, 10% expert park. 1 quad chair, 3 triple chairs, 1 beginner double chair, 3 surface tows.

❑ SKI LODGE - 45,000 square ft. day lodge with self service restaurant & pizzeria, rentals and shops and ticket sales.

❑ LODGING & ACCOMMODATIONS - Condominiums next to the slopes, B&B's, cabins, motels, resort hotels.

❑ KID'S SNOW CAMP - All day supervision includes four hours of instruction and lunch. ages 4-12.

❑ KIDS FUN PARK - Kids can learn & improve their skills while enjoying time in the Kids' Fun Park. Our expanded Snow Park for youngsters features brightly colored foam figures to ski around, a snow tunnel and the cool "Wonder Carpet", an 80 foot moving sidewalk on the snow.

LINCOLN PIONEER VILLAGE & MUSEUM
416 Main Street (Rockport City Park, at west end of Main)
Rockport 47635

❑ Phone: (812) 649-4215
Web: www.spencerco.org/village/village.cfm

❑ Hours: Saturday 10:00am-5:00pm, Sunday 1:00-5:00pm (April-August) and by appointment (Wednesday-Friday).

❑ Admission: $2.00 suggested donation.

The Lincoln Pioneer Village Museum houses hundreds of fascinating artifacts from the area's historic past including a hutch made by Abraham Lincoln's father, Thomas. Located next to the museum is the historic Lincoln Pioneer Village, consisting of cabins that are replicas from the Lincoln era in Spencer County (cabins may be seen on weekends or, by appointment- including the law office, schoolhouse, church, store and typical cabin homes).

HOLIDAY WORLD THEME PARK AND SPLASHIN' SAFARI

452 East Christmas Blvd. (7 miles South of I-64, exit 63, Highway 162), **Santa Claus** 47579

- ❑ Phone: (877) GO-FAMILY
  Web: www.holidayworld.com
- ❑ Hours: Holiday World opens 10:00am. Splashin' Safari 11:00 am. Closing varies by season. (May to mid-October)
- ❑ Admission: General range $26.00-34.00 (age 3+).
- ❑ Miscellaneous: Season passes and 2-day passes save money. Charge cards taken.

HOLIDAY WORLD is consistently rated as one of the cleanest amusement parks in the mid-West. In addition, visitors are entitled to free soft drinks, free sunscreen, and a chance to meet Santa at his summer home. Included in admission are Live shows (country, pop, high dive); Raging Rapids whitewater rafting ride; Spin-dry on Revolution; The Raven; The Legend or the Howlert coasters; Frightful Falls log flume ride; Costumed characters roam about in Holidog's Funtown; and Banshee six story weightlessness ride. Santa appears daily-look for him mostly in Rudolph's Ranch Kiddie Park.

SPLASHIN' SAFARI is where Certified lifeguards oversee fun areas like: Monsoon Lagoon - a 12 level interactive area with water effects, body slides and the GIANT bucket; Congo River tube float; Zoombabwe - the largest waterslide in the world; Watubee whitewater ride; Speed slide; two wave pools (one small, one huge); covered slide; and Crocodile Isle - scaled-down pool and slides for the younger set. Jungle Racer, the first 10-lane racing slide complex ever built, is a water slide so you're guaranteed to cool off even if you're in hot competition with other sliders! The new Jungle Jets area features 163 water elements, such as geysers and drenching spray arches.

For updates, visit our website: www.KidsLoveTravel.com

MARTIN STATE FOREST

PO Box 599 (4 miles east of Shoals, Indiana on U.S. Highway 50)

Shoals 47581

❑ Phone: (812) 247-3491.

www.state.in.us/dnr/forestry/stateforests/martin.htm

Martin State Forest offers a variety of educational opportunities through its woodland management trail and arboretum. The forest features rugged hills, deep woods and long hiking trails. The Arboretum Trail (.25 mile easy) is an informal arboretum (a place for the study and exhibition of trees) was established in an existing wooded area. The collection currently contains about 60 different species identified by signs along the trail. The goal of the Martin State Forest Hoosier Woodland Arboretum is to offer a representation of the common woodland trees of Indiana. Martin State Forest offers 7 miles of mountain bike trails.

FLOOD WALL MURAL AT SUNSET PARK

Sunset Park, Ohio River (Washington & 7th Street)

Tell City 47586

❑ Phone: (812) 547-7933

www.perrycountyindiana.org/attract/floodwall.html

Sunset park contains a painted mural on the flood wall. It was done in sections and took 3 years to paint. It is a rendition of early days of Perry County. Each building, boat and person has historical significance. Each of ten panels has a theme such as manufacturing, lifestyle (residences), mills, banks, merchants and steamboats.

GEORGE ROGERS CLARK NATIONAL HISTORIC PARK

401 South 2nd Street (downtown, just blocks from waterfront)

Vincennes 47591

- ❑ Phone: (812) 882-1776, **Web: www.nps.gov/gero**
- ❑ Hours: Daily 9:00am-5:00pm. Closed Thanksgiving, Christmas, New Years.
- ❑ Admission: $3.00 adult (age 17+) - 7 Days. An optional $4.00 family permit is available for immediate family use.

The site of a little-known, but extremely important, battle that occurred during the Revolutionary War. On February 25, 1779 Virginian George Rogers Clark, with his small army of American frontiersmen and French inhabitants, captured Fort Sackville from the British. Clark's victory aided the United States in laying claim to the vast region that later became the Old Northwest Territory. Today a massive granite-and-marble memorial, more than 80 feet high, stands on the location of Fort Sackville and pays tribute to Clark and his men. Inside are Clark's words carved into Indiana limestone "Great things have been effected by a few men well conducted." Within the visitor center view a 30-minute movie "Long Knives" and look over a few mannequin exhibits. Costumed living history programs are randomly offered.

GROUSELAND

3 West Scott Street (Downtown at Park and Scott Streets)

Vincennes 47591

- ❑ Phone: (812) 882-2096
  Web: www.grouselandfoundation.org
- ❑ Hours: Monday-Saturday 9:00am-5:00pm, Sunday 11:00-5:00pm. (except January, February- daily 11:00am-4:00pm)
- ❑ Admission: $5.00 adult, $2.00-$3.00 child (age 6+)

For updates, visit our website: www.KidsLoveTravel.com

❑   Tours: Ring the doorbell and a guide will escort you in.

The Home of William Henry Harrison, the first Governor of the Indiana Territory and later the 9th President of the United States. He died in office 31 days after his inauguration - some say unnecessarily due to blood letting. The dining room has a bullet hole in the window shutter where someone tried to shoot Harrison (they missed!). As you walk from upstairs down to the warming kitchen (do you know what a buttery is?), you'll see a cutaway of original flooring used in the home. The layers of clay and straw underneath wood provided insulation and noise protection (Harrison didn't want servants to eavesdrop). Stories for the kids include the "giant travel chest" and a Mother's apron needle used for more than sewing. Mr. Harrison is best known for his campaign against Tecumseh - The Treaty of Grouseland was signed at his home.

INDIANA MILITARY MUSEUM

4305 Old Bruceville Road

Vincennes 47591

❑   Phone: (812) 882-8668 or (800) 886-6443
      **www.vincennes.com/History/Military_Museum/military
      _museum.html**

❑   Hours: Daily Noon-5:00pm. Winter hours vary. Its outdoor
      static displays may be viewed from 8:00am-5:00pm daily.

❑   Admission: $2.00 adult, $1.00 student.

❑   Tours: Guided tours only by arrangement.

Military history from the Civil War to Desert Storm. Outdoors - tanks, artillery, helicopters. Indoors - uniforms, flags, relics from battlefields, captured enemy souvenirs, World War II toys and homefront items.

INDIANA TERRITORY CAPITOL VILLAGE

1 West Harrison Street (from US 41, enter town at Sixth St. Head
south to College Ave. Turn right. Follow signs)

Vincennes 47591

❑ Phone: (812) 882-7472

www.in.gov/ism/HistoricSites/Vincennes/Historic.asp

❑ Hours: Tuesday-Saturday 9:00am-5:00pm, Sunday 1:00-
5:00pm (April-late November). Closed winters.

❑ Admission: Donations, please.

❑ Tours: Begin at Log Cabin Visitor's Center

❑ Miscellaneous: Videotape of Vincennes' history in the
Visitor's Center. OLD FRENCH HOUSE AND INDIAN
MUSEUM is nearby and exhibits pioneer life including
influences of early inhabitants, American Indian tribes.

Start at the oldest major government building in the Midwest
- the Indiana Territory Capitol Building. Then, stop in for a
demonstration of old-fashioned printing presses at the Elias
Stout Print Shop…a replica print shop where they first
printed the Law of the Territory and the first Territory
newspaper, "The Indiana Gazette." Learn where we got the
phrase, "UPPER CASE or capital letters" and "mind your
P's and Q's". Lastly, step inside Maurice Thompson's
birthplace where the author of "Alice of Old Vincennes" (a
best-selling romance novel) was born. It features frame
construction, instead of logs, and a cast iron stove in place of
a drafty fireplace - both modern for the time. This is a
volunteer-lead village and, if you plan it right, you'll come
during peak times when all the "villagers" are bustling about
their chores or reenacting major Territory events.

DAVIESS COUNTY MUSEUM

Old Jefferson School (CR 150 South. Off SR 57)

Washington 47501

❑ Phone: (812) 254-5122

Web: www.honest-abe.com/museum/

❑ Hours: Tuesday-Saturday 11:00am-3:00pm (October-April). Tuesday-Saturday 11:00am-4:00pm (May-September).

❑ Admission: Small (ages 12 +)

❑ Miscellaneous: Schools in area. Victorian furnishings and dolls, old license plates, church room, railroad room, medical room (early x-ray machine), military room, beauty/barber chair.

Chapter 9

Seasonal & Special Events

*Note: **Pioneer Encampments** are listed in the back of this section.*

JANUARY

BROWN COUNTY WINTER HIKE

C – Nashville, Brown County State Park. (812) 988-6406 or **www.in.gov/dnr/parklake/parks/brownco.html**. The event features two separate trails for enjoying wildlife, peace and solitude…a day to toss off those winter blahs. Exercise your body and mind with knowledgeable naturalists located throughout the hike to offer interpretive info and answer questions about the park. A special Hiker's Buffet Luncheon – featuring hot, hearty, home-cooked food- will be available at the Abe Martin Lodge. State Park fee. (Saturday after New Years)

KIL-SO-QUEST SLED DOG RACE

NE – Huntington. Reservoir & Kilso-Quah Campground. (800) 848-4282. Indiana's only sled dog race! 2,3,4 and 6 dog races. No admission. (third weekend in January)

FEBRUARY / MARCH

MAPLE SYRUP FESTIVALS

Learn how maple syrup is made from tree tapping to evaporator demonstrations. Taste sampling of food with syrup like pancakes and kettle popcorn. Pioneer music and games.

- ❑ **CW – Rockville**. Parke County Fairgrounds and Billie Creek Village. (765) 569-3430 or **www.billiecreek.org**. Admission. (End of February/beginning of March)
- ❑ **CW – Terre Haute**. Prairie Creek Park Log Cabin. (812) 462-3391. FREE (month long in February thru early March)

❑   **NC – Wakarusa**. Downtown. (574) 862-4344. FREE
    (third or fourth Friday / Saturday in April)
❑   **NE – LaGrange**. Maplewood Nature Center. (260) 463-
    4022. Admission. (third weekend in March)
❑   **SE – Salem**. Sugarbush Farm. (812) 967-4491 or
    www.lmsugarbush.com. FREE
❑   **SW - Evansville**. Wesselman Woods Nature Preserve.
    (812) 479-0771. Admission. (early March weekend)

ST. PATRICK'S DAY CELEBRATIONS

On or the week before St. Patrick's Day see a downtown
lunchtime parade. "Wearin of the green" celebrations include
Irish Dancing, food and music. No Admission.

❑   Participating towns: **Indianapolis, Ireland, Rising Sun,
    South Bend, Terre Haute**.

APRIL

EASTER EGG HUNTS

Egg hunts, party with Easter Bunny, egg decorating contests,
Easter Bonnet contests. No Admission. Participating towns:

❑   **C – Indianapolis** Parks & Rec. (317) 327-0000;
❑   **CE – Connersville**, Whitewater Valley RR Easter Bunny
    Express. **www.whitewatervalleyrr.org**. Admission.
❑   **CW – Cloverdale**, Cagles Mill Lake (765) 795-4576;
❑   **NW – Crown Point**, Old Lake County Courthouse lawn.
    www.crownpoint.net.
❑   **SE – Vevay** (800) HELLO-VV
❑   **SW – Montgomery**, Gasthof Amish Village, CR 650E.
    (812) 486-2600. **www.gastofamishvillage.com**.

MAY

500 FESTIVALS, THE

(Activities to celebrate the Indy 500 Race), **www.500festival.com**.

❑ **C – Anderson**. ANDERSON LITTLE 500 FESTIVAL & RACE. Various locations. (765) 640-2437. Big wheel race, concert, fireworks, sprint car race. Admission. (week before Memorial Day)

❑ **C – Indianapolis**. BANK ONE FESTIVAL & KIDS DAY. Monument Circle. (800) 638-4296. The city's largest outdoor festival for children with Big Wheel races (ages 2-5), carnival, arts and crafts, prizes. No Admission. except for race registrants. (Saturday before Memorial Day weekend)

❑ **C – Indianapolis**. 500 FESTIVAL COMMUNITY DAY. Motor Speedway. (317) 614-6124. Lap the track in your own vehicle. See Pit Row, Gasoline Alley, and the Tower Terrace. Driver's and mechanic's autographs. Admission. (Thursday before race)

❑ **C – Indianapolis**. 500 FESTIVAL PARADE. Downtown. (800) 638-4296. Drivers, floats, marching bands, celebrities. Admission for reserved seating. (Noon the day before race)

❑ **C – Indianapolis**. INDIANAPOLIS 500 MILE RACE. Motor Speedway. (800) 638-4296. The world's largest one-day sporting event. Admission. (Memorial Day)

FAMILY FUN FESTIVAL

NW – Cutler. Adams Mill. (765) 463-7893. Mill tours, old-fashioned games, hayrides, pony rides. FREE. (mid-month Sunday in May)

WHISTLE STOP DAYS

NW – Hesston. Hesston Steam Museum. (219) 872-5055. Ride three steam railroads, visit operating steam sawmill, steam crane, steam power plant and more. FREE. (Memorial Day Weekend)

HARRISON COUNTY POPCORN FESTIVAL

SE – Corydon. Courthouse Square. (888) 738-2137. Celebrate the county's popcorn industry (and the home of popular Cousin Willie's Popcorn). Parade, popcorn demos and contests, popcorn-related foods and some star entertainer. FREE. (mid-month weekend in May)

WINGS OVER MUSCATATUCK

SE – Seymour. Muscatatuck Nat'l Wildlife Refuge, I-65 & US 50. (812) 522-4352. Indiana's only International Migratory Bird Festival – celebrating birds and the natural environment. Field trips, guided bird walks, bird crafts, bird photography, bird calling, tracking, puppet shows. Admission for field trips. (second long weekend in May)

JUNE

STRAWBERRY FESTIVALS

Sample strawberry treats like fresh strawberry shortcakes and strawberry ice cream or sundaes. Entertainment. Kids activities. Most occur in June – some late May.

- ❑ **CE – Metamora.** Along the canal. (765) 647-2109. www.metamora.com. FREE. (first weekend in June)
- ❑ **CW – Crawfordsville.** Historic Lane Place. (800) 866-3973. www.crawfordsville.org. FREE. (second weekend in June)
- ❑ **CW – Terre Haute.** Downtown. (812) 232-8880. Admission. (third Saturday in June)
- ❑ **NC – Wabash.** Historic Downtown. Very Berry Strawberry Fest. (260) 563-0975. FREE. (second Saturday in June)
- ❑ **SE – Starlight.** St. John's Church. (502) 639-9129. FREE. (last Saturday in May)

June *(cont.)*

BILL MONROE MEMORIAL BEAN BLOSSOM BLUEGRASS FESTIVAL

C – Bean Blossom. Bluegrass Hall or Fame Museum. (800) 414-4677. **www.beanblossom.com.** The longest continuously running bluegrass festival in the world, held outdoors with six days of the best in bluegrass, featuring 25 bands, band contest, artist workshops, crafts, children's workshops, pickin' and jammin', food. Camping, cabin rentals, fishing and hiking trails available. Admission. (third week in June)

ITALIAN STREET FESTIVAL

C – Indianapolis. Holy Rosary Church. (317) 636-4778. More than 25 Italian meats, pastas, salads, desserts. Church tours, entertainment. Admission. (first full weekend in June)

INDIAN MARKET

C – Indianapolis. Eiteljorg Museum. (800) 622-2024 or **www.eiteljorg.org.** Show and sale of authentic, hand-made Native American art and food, stories, dance groups and musical performances. Admission. (last weekend in June)

MIDDLE EASTERN FESTIVAL

C– Indianapolis. St. George Orthodox Church. (317) 547-9356. Authentic food, dancing, music, cultural displays, cooking demos, tours. Admission. (second weekend in June)

WILBUR WRIGHT FESTIVAL

CE – Millville. Wilbur Wright Birthplace & Museum, CR 750 East. **www.wilburwrightbirthplace.com.** (765) 332-2495. Home tours, outdoor life-size replica of the 1903 Wright Flyer, live entertainment, flea market, car show, sky divers, kite flying, remote-controlled planes, tours, beans and cornbread. Pork chop dinner Saturday. Admission. (third weekend in June)

TASTE OF TIPPECANOE

CW – Lafayette. Downtown, Riehle Plaza. (765) 423-2787. www.lafayette-in.com. Outdoor festival featuring six stages with live entertainment, 30 local restaurant vendors, Kid's Taste area, fireworks. Admission. (third Saturday in June)

GLASS FESTIVAL

NC – Greentown. Downtown. (765) 628-7818. This town's birthday features tours of the glass factory (see rare Chocolate Glass – invented here), re-enactors, historical displays, children's activities, food, music, historical play. FREE. (second weekend in June)

EGG FESTIVAL

NC– Mentone. Menser Park. (574) 353-7417. The egg basket of the Midwest features the incredible edible egg in a parade, tractor pull, crafts, variety show. FREE. (first weekend in June)

COLE PORTER FESTIVAL

NC – Peru. Miami County Museum. (765) 473-9183. Cole Porter is celebrated as a native of this town with musical entertainment, memorabilia display, birthday cake and van tours. FREE. (second Saturday in June)

ROUND BARN FESTIVAL

NC – Rochester. Downtown, Main Street. (574) 224-2666. Bus tour of round barns and one-room school, bed races, rodeo, parade, kiddy races, wall rock climbing, food, entertainment, games. FREE. (second weekend in June).

CITY OF LAKES BALLOONFEST

NC – Warsaw. Central Park, Winona Lake, and other locations. (800) 800-6090. Hot air balloons, evening balloon glow, sailboat regatta, concerts, fireworks, food. FREE. (last weekend in June)

June *(cont.)*

GERMANFEST

NE – Fort Wayne. Headwaters Park Festival Center. (800) 767-7752 or **www.wunderbar.org.** German heritage celebrated with folk music, dancing, food, kindertag, sports, exhibitions. Admission. (second week of June)

INDIANA HIGHLAND GAMES

NE – Fort Wayne. Zollner Stadium. (800) 767-7752. Sheep herding, bagpipes, Scottish dancing and food, competitions. Admission. (second Saturday in June)

GREEK FESTIVAL

NE – Fort Wayne. Headwaters Park. (260) 489-0774. Greek food, music, dancing and art. Admission. (last weekend in June)

GAELIC FEST

NW – Valparaiso. Sunset Hill Farm. (219) 465-3586. Irish and Scottish celebration. Dance, music, food and arts/crafts. Admission. (second or third Saturday in June)

DAVIESS COUNTY FAIR

SW – Elnora. Fairgrounds off SR57. (812) 692-5831. Family fun including demolition derbies, motorcycle thrill show, western horse show, rides, food, and nightly entertainment. (last week of June)

JULY

JULY 4TH CELEBRATIONS

Live entertainment, parade, carnival, food, fireworks.

- ❑   **C – Fishers.** A Glorious Fourth. Conner Prairie. (317) 776-6000 or **www.connerprairie.org.** Reading of the Declaration of Independence. Admission.
- ❑   **C – Indianapolis.** Fourth Fest. Downtown (317) 633-6363. FREE

- ❑ **C – Indianapolis.** Ice Cream Social. President Benjamin Harrison's Home. (317) 631-1898. Period costumed characters roam the grounds and talk to you. Admission.
- ❑ **CE – Metamora.** Old Fashioned 4th of July. Main Street. (765) 647-2109. FREE.
- ❑ **CW – Lafayette, West Lafayette.** Downtown and 9th Street Hill Historic district. (800) 872-6648. Flag parade, cannon firings.
- ❑ **CW – Rockville.** July 4th Ice Cream Social. Billie Creek Village. (765) 569-3430. Grand cake walk. Admission.
- ❑ **NC – Elkhart.** Sky Concert. (800) 377-3579.
- ❑ **NC – Marion.** Matter Park Shelter. (765) 668-4453. Cruise-in.
- ❑ **NE – Garrett.** Heritage Days. (260) 357-3133. Railroad Museum. (July 3rd & 4th)
- ❑ **NE – Geneva,** Amishville USA. (260) 589-3536.
- ❑ **NE – Huntington.** Forks of Wabash. (260) 356-1903.
- ❑ **NW – Crown Point. www.cpjuly4.com.** Doll and pet parade.
- ❑ **NW – LaPorte.** Jaycees' 4th of July Celebration. (219) 324-5392. Over 50 years with fly over of military jets. Admission. Weeklong.
- ❑ **NW – Wolcott.** Wolcott House Grounds. (219) 279-2123. FREE. (July 3rd & 4th)
- ❑ **SE – Corydon.** Old Settlers Day. Old Capitol Square. (812) 738-4890. Pioneer demonstrations. No Admission.
- ❑ **SW – Evansville.** Freedom Festival. Downtown riverfront. **www.evansvillefreedomfestival.org.** (812) 434-4848. Thunder on the Ohio, Thunder Air, Hot Air Balloons. Admission. (five day event)

July *(cont.)*

SCOTTISH FESTIVAL

C – Columbus. Mill Race Park. **www.scottishfestival.org**. (800) 468-6564 or Bagpipe bands, sheepdog trials, Highland dancing, athletic competitions and traditional foods. Admission. (third weekend in July)

HOT DOG FESTIVAL

C – Frankfort. Courthouse Square. (765) 654-4081. Hot dogs with every topping imaginable! Puppy Park with children's activities and other "dog" related events. FREE. (last weekend in July)

ELKHART COUNTY 4-H FAIR

NC – Goshen, County Fairgrounds. (574) 533-3247 or **www.4hfair.org**. One of the largest county fairs in the nation with 4-H exhibits, demos, food, carnival and free top-name entertainment. Admission. (July)

HAYNES-APPERSON FESTIVAL

NC – Kokomo. Downtown. (800) 456-1106. The town celebrates its automotive history with Haynes Museum tours, car shows, a parade, carnival, food, and talent contest. FREE. (first weekend in July)

CIRCUS CITY FESTIVAL

NC – Peru. Circus City Festival Arena. (765) 472-3918 or **www.perucircus.com**. Best amateur youth performances include flying trapeze, high wire, bareback riding. Carnival downtown. Tour Hall of Fame, rides, food. Admission. (third week of July)

SWISS DAYS

NE – Berne. Downtown. **www.berneswissdays.com**. (260) 589-8080. Yodeling, folk dancing, concerts, cheese making factory tours, Swiss food and famous apple dumplings. FREE. (last weekend in July)

THREE RIVERS FESTIVAL

NE – Fort Wayne. Headwaters Park. (260) 426-5556 or **www.threeriversfestival.org**. Children's Fest, McDonald's Parade, music, raft race, fireworks. Admission to some events. (mid-month, weeklong in July)

LAGRANGE COUNTY 4-H FAIR

NE – LaGrange, County Fairgrounds. (260) 768-4165. 4-H shows and midway. Admission per carload. (mid-month for one week in July)

GREAT MILL RACE

NW – Cutler. Adam's Mill. (765) 463-7893. Boat races every half hour; crafts, displays, mill tours and demonstrations, food. FREE. (second Saturday in July)

STARKE COUNTY 4-H FAIR

NW – Hamlet. Fairgrounds (500N & 600E). (219) 772-9141. Projects, posters, animal shows, livestock sale, talent show, carnival, food, games, demonstrations. FREE. (third week in July)

PORTER COUNTY FAIR

NW – Valparaiso. Fairgrounds. **www.portercofair.org**. Expo Center. (last part of month in July)

PIEROGI FESTIVAL

NW – Whiting. Historic Downtown. (219) 659-0292. Slovak and Polish delicacies, music, dancing, parade. FREE. (last weekend in July)

July *(cont.)*

HARRISON COUNTY FAIR

SE – Corydon. County Fairgrounds. Carnival food and rides, livestock shows, animal exhibits, horse racing, grandstand shows, demolition derbies and tractor pulls. (end of July, beginning of August for one week)

MADISON REGATTA

SE – Madison. Ohio River. **www.madisonregatta.com**. (812) 265-5000. Races featuring the world's fastest boats-unlimited hydroplanes. Also balloon race, parade, music, fireworks. Some events have admission. (July 4th week)

FLOYD COUNTY FAIR

SE – New Albany. Floyd County Fairgrounds, 2818 Green Valley Road. (812) 948-5470. Carnival and 4-H exhibits (open at 6:00pm daily). Also donkey race, livestock, rodeo and grandstand events. (weekend after July 4th for six days)

SCOTT COUNTY 4-H FAIR

SE – Scottsburg, County Fairgrounds. (812) 752-8450. Parade, races, 4-H exhibits, shows, rides and food. (mid-month for one week in July)

LIMESTONE HERITAGE FESTIVAL

SW – Bedford. Brian Lane Way. (800) 798-0969. An important Indiana resource, Bedford stone was used to build the Empire State Building and the Pentagon. Quarry tours, parade, fireworks, sculpture exhibits and competition. No Admission. (week up to July 4th)

VANDERBURGH COUNTY FAIR

SW – Evansville. 4-H Fairgrounds. (812) 868-0636. Exhibits, entertainment, food, rides. Admission. (last week in July)

GIBSON COUNTY FAIR

SW – Princeton. Fairgrounds. **www.gibsoncountyfair.com.** (812) 385-3445. Animals exhibits, tractor pulls, horse shows, live entertainment, kids circus, carnival and demolition derbies. (begins Sunday after the 4th for one week in July)

AUGUST

GLASS FESTIVAL

C – Elwood. Callaway Park. (765) 552-0180 or **www.elwood.org/glassfestival/.** Glass factory tours include: Prestige Art Glass, SR 13 (765) 552-0688; Spencers Lapidary (marbles), SR 37 & SR 13 (765) 552-0784; The House of Glass, SR 28 (765) 552-6841. Food, carnival, volksmarch, parade. FREE. (third weekend in August)

INDIANA STATE FAIR

C – Indianapolis. State Fairgrounds. (317) 927-7500 or **www.indianastatefair.com.** Indiana's best exhibitors, competitors and entertainers are joined by top national entertainment. Blue ribbon agricultural exhibits, top Indiana youth exhibitors. Hours 6:00am to late evening. Admission. (middle of August for 11 days)

SUMMER HEAT

CE – Muncie. County Airport. (765) 284-2700. See 45 hot air balloons rise along with air shows, entertainment. Admission.   (second weekend, Thursday – Saturday in August)

GENE STRATTON-PORTER CHAUTAUQUA DAYS

NE – Rome City. Sylvan Lake. (260) 854-3790. Tea party, Birthday party in Cabin, lake cruises, tours of GSP's (famous author and nature photographer) lovely home and property, food, entertainment. Admission. (mid-month weekend in August)

August *(cont.)*

WHEELS OF YESTERYEAR ANTIQUE POWER SHOW & PIONEER FESTIVAL

NE – Bluffton. (260) 565-3217. Pre-1840 encampment, pioneer crafts, antique tractor and engine show. Tractor pulls, flea market and auction. FREE. (mid-August weekend)

INDIAN POW-WOW

NE – Columbia City. Mihsihkinaahkwa Pow Wow Morsches Park. (260) 244-7843. Authentic Native American music and dance. Food (buffalo), storytelling, traditional crafts, and historical language. Admission. (second weekend in August)

FT. WAYNE RAILROAD HISTORICAL OPEN HOUSE

NE – New Haven. 15808 Edgerton Rd. (260) 493-0765. Home to steam locomotive 765, a smaller switching steam locomotive, two wooden cabooses, a 200-ton wrecker, a diesel locomotive and other historic railroad equipment. You can tour the facility and talk to the people who maintain and operate this historic rail equipment, sit in the engineer's seat of a 400-ton iron horse and get a conductor's eye view from a 100-year-old caboose. Take a 20-minute ride in a vintage caboose. (August)

PICKLE FEST

NE – St. Joe. (State Route 1, off I-69 & Dupont) (260) 337-5461 or **www.stjoepicklefestival.com**. Start with a pickle factory tour. Pickle Derby, Pickle People Contest, variety of children's activities (including a large petting zoo), great entertainment, fireworks, and a huge craft tent. FREE. (second full weekend in August)

LAKE COUNTY FAIR

NW – Crown Point. **www.crownpoint.net.** As Indiana's largest county fair, the Lake County Fair proudly hosts 4-H displays, agricultural showcases, entertainment events, food and craft booths. (beginning first Friday in August for 9 days)

POTATO FEST

NW – Medaryville. Downtown. (219) 843-3371. Spuds with every imaginable topping, curly fries, numerous potato creations. FREE. (mid-month weekend in August)

DAN PATCH DAYS

NW – Oxford. Rommel Park. (765) 385-2251. Rodeo, draft horse pull, Dan Patch memorabilia (famous pacer horse), parade, entertainment, bingo. Admission. (second weekend in August)

STRASSENFEST

SW – Jasper. Downtown. (812) 482-6866 or (800) 968-4578. **www.jasperstrassenfest.org.** German heritage with music, food, talent show. Admission. (first weekend in August)

SCHWEIZER FEST

SW – Tell City, Hall Park. (888) 343-6262. Swiss-German heritage celebration offering free entertainment, authentic food, rides and market. FREE. (second week in August)

WATERMELON FESTIVAL

SW – Vincennes. Downtown. (812) 882-6440. Free watermelon, food sidewalk sales, sports competition, games pageants, historic site tours. (first weekend in August)

SEPTEMBER

INDIAN POW-WOWS

A day to hear drums, smell fry bread, watch dancers, listen to tales, and visit tents of Native American traders. Traditional arts, clothing, language & history.

- ❑ **C – Anderson**. Andersontown PowWow and Indian Market. **www.andersontownpowwow.com**. (765) 643-5633. (weekend after Labor Day)
- ❑ **CW – Attica**. Potawatomi Festival. Wabash riverfront. (765) 764-4943. Admission. (third weekend in September)
- ❑ **CW – Terre Haute**. Gathering of the People Pow Wow. Vigo County Conservation Club grounds. (812) 219-3979. Admission. (last weekend in September)
- ❑ **SW – Evansville**. Native American Days. Angel Mounds. (812) 853-3956. FREE. (last weekend in September)

THE GREEK FESTIVAL

C – Indianapolis, Holy Trinity Greek Orthodox Church. 317-283-3816 has been an Indianapolis tradition for 31 years. Always the weekend after Labor Day. Come join us rain or shine for music, food and dancing. Enjoy traditional Greek music by the Bill Simons band, home made pastries, traditional Greek foods. Admission. (weekend after Labor Day)

LITTLE ITALY FESTIVAL

CW – Clinton. Water Street. (765) 832-6606 or **www.littleitalyfestival.org**. Italian music and authentic food. Spaghetti-eating contest, grape stomping. FREE. (Labor Day Weekend)

OLD JAIL MUSEUM BREAKOUT

CW – Crawfordsville. Old Jail Museum. (800) 866-3973. See the only rotary jail built in Indiana (cells turn every half hour). Music, entertainment, children's events, free refreshments. FREE. (Labor Day)

CULTURE, ARTS & CUISINE CELEBRATION

CW – Terre Haute. Fairbanks Park. (812) 232-2727. Sample the world through ethnic displays, costumes, music, dance and foods. FREE. (fourth weekend in September)

GLOBAL FEST

CW – West Lafayette. Morton community Center. (765) 775-5120. Celebrate the city's many cultures with international foods, cultural displays, dance, music. FREE. (Labor Day Weekend)

FAIRMONT MUSEUM DAYS FESTIVAL

NC – Fairmount. Main Street. (765) 948-4555 or **www.jamesdeanartifacts.com**. Tour Fairmount Historical Museum/James Dean Museum. Parade, look-alike contest, entertainment with 50's music, dance contest, all James Dean movies playing, plus recognition of hometowner, Jim Davis' "Garfield" series. FREE. (last weekend in September)

BLUEBERRY FESTIVAL

NC – Plymouth. Marshall County. Centennial Park. (888) 936-5020 or **www.blueberryfestival.org**. Largest 3 day festival in Indiana with blueberry treats like milkshakes, pie and ice cream. Parade, circus, fireworks, fair food. FREE. (Labor Day Weekend)

September *(cont.)*

PUMPKIN TRAINS

NC – Wakarusa. Old Railroad. (574) 862-2714. Take a mini train ride to the patch and pick a free pumpkin. Admission. (September / October)

AUBURN-CORD DUESENBERG FESTIVAL

NE – Auburn. (260) 925-3600 or www.acdfestival.org. Classic car showcase. Parade of Classics, automotive museums, entertainment and a kids art tent. Admission. (Labor Day Weekend)

MARSHMALLOW FESTIVAL

NE – Ligonier. Main Street. (260) 894-9000 or **www.marshmallowfestival.com**. The country's center for marshmallow making. Bake-off, marshmallow putting contest, games, rides, entertainment, parade, area factory history. FREE. (Labor Day Weekend)

WIZARD OF OZ FESTIVAL

NW – Chesterton. Downtown. (219) 926-7048 or **www.yellowbrickroadonline.com**. Oz Fantasy Museum tours, look-alike contests, meet some of the actual MGM Munchkins. FREE. (third weekend in September)

STEAM & POWER SHOW

NW – Hesston. Steam Museum. (219) 872-5055. Rated Top 10 Festival. Steam train rides across 155 scenic acres. Also see restored steam power plant, sawmill, antique engines, tractors. Admission. (Labor Day Weekend)

OKTOBERFEST

NW – LaPorte. Fairgrounds. (219) 874-8927. International food, artistry, entertainment like dancing and music, rides. Admission. (Labor Day Weekend)

BALLOONFEST

NW – Valparaiso. Porter county Fairgrounds. (219) 462-1209. 20 some balloons with launch and glows, food, souvenirs. Admission. (first weekend after Labor Day)

POPCORN FESTIVAL

NW – Valparaiso. Downtown. www.popcornfest.org. (219) 464-8332. In honor of the late Orville Redenbacher and his origin from this town. Popcorn parade, hot air balloon show, children's play areas, food, live entertainment. FREE. (first weekend after Labor Day)

FOSSIL FEST

SE – Clarksville. Falls of the Ohio State Park. (812) 280-9970. Special exhibits, guest speakers, fossil & mineral dealers, children's activity area and fossil collection piles donated by Liter's Quarry. (third weekend in September)

PUMPKIN SHOW

SE – Versailles. Courthouse Square. (812) 689-6188. Carnival, concessions, contest, entertainment, parade. Giant pumpkin weighing & pumpkin foods. FREE. (last weekend in September)

PUMPKIN FESTIVAL

SW – French Lick. Downtown, Maple St & SR56. (812) 936-2405. Big Pumpkin Parade, carnival, food. FREE. (last week in September to beginning of October)

TURKEY TROT FESTIVAL

SW – Montgomery, Ruritan Park, north of Hwy. 50. (812) 254-4544. The nationally known event features many turkey races, live entertainment, bingo, greased pig contests, and food. (first long weekend in September)

SEPTEMBER / OCTOBER

HARVEST FESTIVALS

Horses plow fields, antique tractors, chuckwagon-style dinner, corn shredding, tractor pull, hayrides, corn shucking competition and straw baling.

- ❏ **C – Fishers**. Country Fair. Conner Prairie. (800) 966-1836. Admission. (third weekend in September)
- ❏ **CW – Rockville**. Steam Harvest Days. Billie Creek Village. (765) 569-3430 or **www.billiecreek.org**. Admission. (Labor Day Weekend)
- ❏ **NW – Valparaiso**, Sunset Farm Hill County Park (US 6 & Meridian Road). (219) 465-3586.
- ❏ **NW – Wanatah**. Scarecrow Festival. US 421 & US 30. (219) 733-2183. FREE. (fourth weekend in September)

FALL PLAYLANDS

Corn Mazes, Hayrides, Petting Animals, Pick-a-Pumpkin patches, Scarecrows, Painted Pumpkins, Pumpkin Carving Contests, refreshments and entertainment. Admission.

- ❏ **C – Greenfield**. S&H Campground (2573 W 100 North), Family Pumpkin Patch and Poppin' Corn Maze. (317) 326-4467.
- ❏ **C – Indianapolis**. Waterman's Farm Market. 7010 E. Raymond St. Admission. (317) 356-6995. (October, daily)
- ❏ **C – Noblesville**. Stonycreek Farm. (317) 773-3344 or **www.stonycreekfarm.net**. Admission. (early September-October)
- ❏ **CE – Cambridge City**. Dougherty Orchards. (765) 478-5198 or **www.doughertyorchards.com**. Also, Apple House Tours. Admission. (September – December, Daily)
- ❏ **NC – Goshen**. Kercher's Sunrise Orchards. CR 38. (574) 533-6311. (Mid-September to Mid-October)

- NC – **Millersburg**. Indiana Maze Plex. 69623 SR 13. (574) 642-5111. (August – October)
- NC - **Peru**. Tate Orchard / Apple Dumpling Inn. (765) 985-2467
- NE – **Fort Wayne** area. JamBam's. Hilger's Farm Market & Restaurant, 13210 W US 30. (888) 932-1827. Rock Climbing Wall, a Power Bounce, and a 200 foot long Corn Snake. Faster Pastor competitions. (weekend after Labor Day – October)
- NE - **Ligonier**. Pumpkin Fantasyland. Fashion Farm, 1680 Lincolnway West. (800) 254-8090. (October)
- NW – **Hobart**. County Line Orchard. (219) 947-4477. (October)
- SE – **Starlight**. Joe Huber Family Farm & Restaurant. 2421 Scottsville Road (I – 64 East to Exit 119). (877) JOE HUBERS or **www.joehubers.com**. Also apple orchard in September (wagon ride to orchard for picking). (September / October)

APPLE FESTIVALS

Apple peeling and pie-eating contests, apple foods demos, apple foods-pies, donuts, cider, butter. Carnival.

- C – **Danville**. Heartland Apple Festival, Beasley's Orchard (Rockville Road just east of downtown Danville). (317) 745-4876 or **www.beasleysorchard.com**. Farming animal shows, puppets, storytelling. $5.00 per vehicle. (first and second weekend in October)
- C - **Pendleton**. Grabow's Orchard. 6397 SR 13 off I-69. (888) 534-3225. Raspberries too! (last Saturday in September)
- C – **Sheridan**. Stuckey Farm Market, (2 ½ miles north of SR32 on County Line Rd). (317) 769-4172. FREE. (June-November, daily except Sunday)

Apple Festivals *(cont.)*

- ❏ **C – Trafalgar**. Apple Works. (I-65 North to US 31 N to CR 250W (south). **www.apple-works.com**. (317) 878-9317. Music, storytelling, wagon rides, petting zoo, scarecrow crafts. (weekends in October)
- ❏ **NC - Nappanee**. (800) 517-9739. 600 lb. Apple pie. FREE. (third weekend in September)
- ❏ **NC – Peru**. McClure's Tate Orchard. (765) 985-2467 or **www.mcclurestateorchard.com**. Apples and dumplings.
- ❏ **NW – Laporte**. Garwood Orchards. (219) 362-4385. (mid-month Saturday in September)
- ❏ **SE – Batesville**. Liberty Park. (812) 933-3103. AppleFest, carriage rides. FREE. (last weekend in September)
- ❏ **SE – Starlight**. Stumler Orchard., 10924 St. John's Road, I-64 west to exit 119. (812) 923-3832. Hayrides to the pumpkin patch. FREE. (first weekend in October)

OKTOBERFEST

German music and dance, food, parade, carnival and hayrides.

- ❏ **SW – Huntingburg**. Herbstfest. City Park at First & Cherry Streets. (812) 683-5699. (first long weekend in October)
- ❏ **SW– New Harmony**. Kunstfest. (800) 231-2168. Petting zoo, wagon rides, general store, historic homes to tour. FREE, some fees for historic tours. (two weekends after Labor Day)
- ❏ **CW – Terre Haute**. Wabash Valley Fairgrounds, US 41 South. (812) 466-2107. Admission (12+). (first two Saturdays in October)

OCTOBER

RILEY FESTIVAL

C – Greenfield. Downtown. (317) 462-2141. Commemorate James Whitcomb Riley's birthday. Parades, entertainment, pumpkin contest, food. FREE. (October, first Thursday – Sunday)

HOOSIER STORYTELLING FESTIVAL

C – Indianapolis. Indiana Museum and Military Park. (317) 255-7628 or **www.storytellingarts.org/festival.htm**. Annual festival presenting national and regional storytellers performing on multiple stages. Children's Stage, Family Storytelling Activities Tent (crafts, activities and performances to enhance the storytelling experience), Sharing Hoosier History Through Stories, and A Story Cabaret. These tellers from around the country will share music and stories from their childhoods, cultures, and heritages. Admission. (first full week of October, Wednesday-Saturday)

PUMPKIN PATCH TRAIN

CE – Knightstown. Carthage, Knightstown and Shirley Railroad Train. (765) 345-5561. The train stops at a field of pumpkins where the kids can get off the train and find just the right pumpkin for themselves, which they must carry back to the train. Advance reservations. Train admission fees. (October, each weekend).

October *(cont.)*

PARKE COUNTY COVERED BRIDGE FESTIVAL

CW – Ten days in the middle of October. County celebrates Indiana's historic past with 32 Historic Covered Bridges. Hours: 9:00am-6:00pm. FREE. **www.coveredbridges.com.**

❑ **Rockville** – Headquarters. Sample cooking and crafts. Bus tours.

❑ **Billie Creek Village** – America's largest gathering of turn-of-the-century craftsmen. 3 bridges, entertainment, horse-pulled wagon rides, authentic foods and costumes. Admission. BLACK ROUTE.

❑ **Bridgeton** – 245-foot double-span covered bridge above the dam, waterfall near a working gristmill. Weaver, crafters, food. RED ROUTE.

❑ **Mansfield** – Historic Village, 1820's water-powered grist mill, 1867 covered bridge. BLACK ROUTE.

❑ **Mecca** – 2 historic schoolhouses, covered bridge, 1800's outdoor metal jail, old clay tile factory, crafts, foods, and dancing on the bridge. BROWN ROUTE & RED ROUTE.

❑ **Montezuma** – Historic river town and home of the Wabash-Erie Canal bed, Aztec trading post, hog roast, hayrides, trail rides.

❑ **Rosedale** – Potato fields, antique equipment. RED ROUTE.

❑ **Tangier** – 5 covered bridges, serve Tangier's famous "buried roast beef". BLUE & YELLOW ROUTE.

LEWIS AND CLARK RIVER FESTIVAL

SE – **Clarksville**, Falls of the Ohio State Park, George Rogers Clark Homesite. **www.fallsoftheohio.org.** (812) 283-4999. Re-enactors portray William Clark, Meriwether Lewis and George Rogers Clark, and the Lewis and Clark "Corps of Discovery" expedition. They left Mill Creek in Clarksville in 1803 to discover the West. Children's games, craft demos and book signings. (last weekend in October)

NOVEMBER

INTERNATIONAL FESTIVAL

C – **Indianapolis**, West Pavilion, Indiana State Fairgrounds. (317) 236-6515 or **www.indyinternationalfestival.org**. Hosted by The Nationalities Council of Indiana. Event features cultural displays, artist demonstrations, entertainment, ethnic foods, and a global bazaar. Admission. (first long weekend in November)

NOVEMBER / DECEMBER

CHRISTMAS EXPRESS

CE – **Connersville**. Whitewater Valley Railroad. (765) 825-2054 or **www.whitewatervalleyrr.org**. Special holiday shopping excursions to Metamora. Santa Claus rides many of these trains to add to the holiday fun. Early reservations are highly recommended. Admission $8.00-$16.00. (Friday nights, Saturday and Sunday afternoons for the three weekends following Thanksgiving)

WINTER WONDERLAND TRAIN

NC – **Wakarusa**. Old Wakarusa Railroad. (574) 862-2714. Diesel train (mini) ride through decorated trees, bridges, buildings and tunnels with holiday music throughout. 30 minute rides. Dress warmly. (Thanksgiving – first weekend in January)

FESTIVAL OF GINGERBREAD

NE – **Fort Wayne**. Old City Hall Historical Museum. (260) 426-2882. Creations of fantasy gingerbread houses on display. (Children's to Professional categories)   FREE. (Thanksgiving through mid-December)

November / December *(cont.)*

A COURTYARD CHRISTMAS

SE – Scottsburg. Scott County Courthouse Courtyard. (812) 752-4343. 700 plus luminaries glowing, carriage rides, food, entertainment, parade with Santa, children's games and carolers. FREE. (Saturday after Thanksgiving)

HOLIDAY MUSICAL

SE – Starlight. Joe Huber Family Farm and Restaurant. (812) 923-5255 or **www.joehuber.com**. Holiday music. Ticket price includes Huber's famous holiday dinner buffet and show. Adults $34.95, Children (4-10) $14.95. Dinner 6:30, Show 7:30pm. (Thanksgiving weekend thru mid-December)

FESTIVAL OF LIGHTS

Lighted roadways or walkways. Entertainment. Carolers. Santa. Themed with characters and historical events. (Evenings beginning the weekend of Thanksgiving through December unless noted otherwise)

- ❑ **C – Columbus.** Mill Race Park. (800) 468-6564 or **www.columbus.in.us**. Over 2 million lights. Small Admission.
- ❑ **C – Fishers.** Conner Prairie by Candlelight. (800) 966-1836 or **www.connerprairie.org**. Walk-thru a holiday village 1836 and Festival of Gingerbread display. Admission/Reservations. (December, Wednesday-Sunday evenings)
- ❑ **C – Indianapolis.** Christmas at the Zoo. Indianapolis Zoo. (317) 630-2001. 700,000 lights and 180 displays. Train & Trolley Rides. Admission.
- ❑ **CE – Metamora.** Old Fashioned Christmas Walk. (765) 647-6512 or **www.emetamora.com**. Live nativity. Luminaries along roads and canal banks. FREE.

❑ **CE – Muncie.** Minnetrista Cultural Center & Gardens. (765) 282-4848 or **www.mccoak.org**. Luminaria Walk.

❑ **CE – Parker City.** Holiday House of Lights, ME's Zoo. (765) 468-8559 or **www.meszoo.com**.

❑ **NC – Marion.** Christmas City Walkway of Lights, Riverwalk. (800) 662-9474 or **www.walkwayoflights.com**. Walk or drive, Gift shop. Daily. FREE.

❑ **NE – Fort Wayne.** Franke Park. Admission.

❑ **NW – Valparaiso.** Holiday Lights. Sunset Hill Farm County Park, Hwy. 6. (219) 465-3586. (Thanksgiving thru first weekend in December)

❑ **SE – Madison.** Festival of Lights along Vaughn Drive. Donations accepted. (812) 265-3135.

❑ **SE – Rising Sun.** Holiday Winter Walk. Riverfront. (888) RSNG-SUN. Turn of the century light display on the riverfront, Santa's Castle and horse-drawn carriage. FREE. (first weekend in December)

❑ **SW – Evansville.** Fantasy of Lights. Garvin Park. (812)474-2348. Admission.

❑ **SW – Santa Claus.** (812) 937-2848. Tour thru Christmas Lake Village.

FESTIVAL OF TREES

Beautifully decorated trees for sale to benefit charity. Gift shops. Entertainment. (End of November)

❑ **CE – Richmond**, Hayes Arboretum Nature Center. (765) 962-3745 or **www.hayesarboretum.org**.

❑ **NE – Fort Wayne.** Embassy Theatre. (260) 424-4071. Admission.

DECEMBER

HOLIDAY OPEN HOUSES

Holiday decorated historic homes with costumed interpreters and special music and refreshments.

- ❏ **C – Anderson**. Gruenewalt House. (765) 646-5771. (first weekend in December)
- ❏ **C – Indianapolis**. President Benjamin Harrison Home. (317) 631-1888. Family Christmas - meet President Harrison and the household staff in various rooms through the house. Admission. (weekends from Thanksgiving through December)
- ❏ **CE – Cambridge City**. Family Christmas Festival at Huddleston Farmhouse Inn. (765) 478-3172. (Early to mid-December)
- ❏ **CE – Richmond**. Christmas at Wayne County Museum. (765) 962-5756. (first Sunday in December)
- ❏ **CW – Lafayette**. Victorian Christmas Tour of Fowler House, Tippecanoe County Museum. (765) 476-8402 or **www.tcha.mus.in.us**
- ❏ **NC – Bristol**. A Victorian Christmas Celebration. Elkhart County Museum. (574) 848-4322. Many Victorian Christmas characters and meal. Admission. (first or second weekend in December)
- ❏ **NC– Elkhart**. Ruthmere Museum. (800) 517-9737. (first Saturday in December)
- ❏ **NC – Kokomo**. Christmas at the Seiberling Mansion. (765) 452-4314. Admission. (Thanksgiving weekend to third week of December)
- ❏ **NC – South Bend**. Christmas at Copshaholm. (574) 235-9664. Admission. (Thanksgiving weekend to week after New Years)
- ❏ **NE – Geneva**. Limberlost State Historic Site. (260) 368-7428. (second weekend in December)

❑ **NE – Huntington**. Christmas at the Forks. (260) 356-
1903. (first weekend in December)

❑ **NE – Rome City**. Gene-Stratton Porter Home. (260) 854-
3790. (second weekend in November)

❑ **NW – Lowell**. Christmas at Buckley Homestead.
(219) 696-6769. (first weekend in December)

❑ **NW – Michigan City**. Christmas at Barker Mansion, 631
Washington St. (219) 873-1520. Admission. (first
Saturday in December to mid-January)

❑ **NW – Porter**. Christmas in the Dunes. Chellberg Farm &
Bailly Homestead. (219) 926-7561. (second Sunday in
December)

❑ **SE – Aurora**. Hillforest Mansion, 213 Fifth St.. (812) 926-
0087 or **www.dearborncounty.org**. Victorian Christmas.
Admission. (first two weekends in December)

❑ **SE – Vevay**. Over the River and Through the Woods,
Downtown. (800) HELLO-VV. Admission. (first
weekend in December)

❑ **SW – Boonville**. (812) 897-3100. Christmas in Boon
Village and at the Warrick County Museum, decorated.

❑ **SW – Evansville**. Rietz Home. (812) 426-1871.
(Thanksgiving week to Christmas week, daily except
Monday)

❑ **SW – Gentryville**. Christmas through the Ages at Col.
William Jones State Historic Site. (812) 937-2802.
(second weekend in December)

❑ **SW – New Harmony**. (812) 682-4488. Historic homes /
village and museum. Admission. (first Saturday in
December)

CIRCLE OF LIGHTS

C – Indianapolis.   Monument Circle.   (317) 237-2222.
Lighting of the "World's Largest Christmas Tree" plus
singing from the Indianapolis Children's Choir.   FREE.
(December, mid-month thru first week of January)

December *(cont.)*

POLAR BEAR EXPRESS

C – Noblesville. Indiana Transportation Museum. (317) 773-6000. Train tickets include a reading and visual presentation of the popular story "The Polar Express", train ride and snacks. Admission and reservations. (December, first two weekends)

PARKE COUNTY COVERED BRIDGE CHRISTMAS

CW – Rockville. Parke County Fairgrounds & other locations. (765) 569-5226. Travel through historic covered bridges and villages decorated for the holidays. Shopping, food. FREE. (December, first full weekend)

CHRISTMAS WALK IN THE PARK

CW – Terre Haute. Fowler Park Pioneer Log Village & Deming Park. (812) 232-2727. Historic village streets and shelters decorated for the holidays, dulcimer music, refreshments. Dress warmly, bring a flashlight. Ride old-fashioned carriages or mini-trains. FREE. (Thanksgiving weekend and first weekend in December)

LIVE NATIVITY SCENE

NE – Shipshewana. Downtown. **www.shipshewana.com**. (260) 768-4163 or Costumed interpreters re-enact and celebrate the birth of Christ. Live animals and caroling too. FREE. (second weekend in December)

SANTA CANDY CANE EXPRESS

NW – Hesston Steam Museum. (219) 872-5055 or **www.hesston.org**. Visit with Santa in his caboose and take a cozy winter train ride in the first class enclosed coach. FREE (first two weekends in December)

LIVE NATIVITY

NW – Valparaiso. Courthouse. (219) 464-8332. Live Nativity with animals. Caroling, carriage rides, refreshments, pictures with Santa. FREE. (first Saturday in December)

HOLLYDAZE

SW – Evansville. Mesker Park Zoo. (812) 435-6143 or **www.meskerparkzoo.com**. Meet zoo critters, create tasty treats for animals, make a take-home craft, and meet Santa and Mrs. Claus. Free drinks and cookies served. Admission. (second weekend in December)

SANTA CLAUS POST OFFICE

SW – Santa Claus. Hwy 162 and 245. (812) 937-4469. Nation's only post office with a "Santa Claus" postmark. (daily except Sunday in December)

NEW YEAR'S EVE CELEBRATION

Non-alcoholic party includes music, dance, clowns, storytellers, magicians, juggling and fireworks.

❑   **C – Indianapolis.** Indiana State Museum. (317) 232-1637. Admission

❑   **NC – Elkhart.** FamilyFest. (800) 262-8161. Admission.

❑   **SW – Evansville.** First Night. (812) 422-2111. Admission.

(Year-long Pioneer Days / Encampments continued on next page)

YEAR LONG

PIONEER DAYS / ENCAMPMENTS

Early 1800's frontier life. Period costumed townsfolk, soldiers, Native Americans. See fur trading posts, kids' infantry, barber shop medicine, and old-fashioned games. Demonstrations of spinning, broom making, dancing, weaving, woodcarving, blacksmiths and tomahawk throwing. Open hearth cooking with period foods for sale like kettle popcorn and chips, cider, stew, barbecue, buffalo burgers, dumplings, apple butter, ham & beans, birch tea and Indian fry bread.

APRIL

MOUNTAIN MEN RENDEZVOUS

CW – Bridgeton. **www.coveredbridges.com**. (765) 548-2136. Located around Parke counties oldest home…the 1822 Case Log Cabin. See the mill in operation (est. 1823) and stroll through the camps. FREE. (last weekend in April)

REDBUD TRAIL RENDEZVOUS

NC – Rochester. **www.icss.net/~fchs/events.htm**. Fulton County Historical Society Grounds. (574) 223-4436. Admission. (April)

MAY

FESTIVAL OF THE WHIPPOORWILL MOON

NE – Huntington. Forks of the Wabash Park. (260) 356-1903. (first weekend in May)

MORGAN'S RAID, SCOTT COUNTY

SE – Lexington, Township Park. (812) 752-7270 or **www.greatscottindiana.org**. Admission. (Memorial Day weekend).

WESSELMAN WOODS NATURE PRESERVE

SW – **Evansville.** (812) 479-0771. (third weekend in May)

SPIRIT OF VINCENNES RENDEZVOUS

SW – **Vincennes.** French Commons. (812) 886-6443 or **www.spiritofvincennes.org.** Battlefield activities of George Rogers Clark. Admission. (Memorial Day weekend)

JUNE

CIVIL WAR DAYS

CW – **Rockville.** Billie Creek Village. (765) 569-3430 or **www.billiecreek.org.** Indiana's largest Civil War reenactment with tractor shuttle from Rockville. Admission. (second weekend in June)

FEAST OF THE WILD ROSE MOON

NC – **Middlebury.** Loveway Horseback Riding Facility. (574) 293-4640. Step back in time as you visit buckskinners and fur traders from the French and Indian War era. Admission. (first weekend in June)

JULY

HOOSIER HISTORY FEST

C – **Indianapolis.** Indiana Historical Society. (317) 232-1882 or **www.indianahistory.org/fest.** Enjoy family activities, historical re-enactors, encampments, exhibitions, music and more while you learn about Indiana's fascinating history. FREE. (last Saturday in July)

OLD CAPITOL DAYS

SE - **Corydon.** First State Office Building lawn. (812) 738-4890. Living history encampments covering periods from 1756-1812. Demonstrations and storytelling each day. FREE. (weekend after the 4th of July)

Pioneer Days / Encampments *(cont.)*

AUGUST

STEAM & GAS SHOW

CW – **Perrysville**. Skinner Farm Museum & Village. SR32W. (765) 793-4079. Admission (third weekend in August)

DAVID ROGERS DAY

NE – **LaGrange**. David Rogers Park. (260) 463-7825. Admission. (late in the month of August)

HAMLET FESTIVAL & RENDEZVOUS

NW – **Hamlet**. 4-H County Fairgrounds. (574) 586-2105. FREE. (third weekend in August)

SEPTEMBER

CIVIL WAR ENCAMPMENT

CE – **Cambridge City**. Huddleston Farmhouse Inn. (765) 478-3172. Admission. (weekend after Labor Day)

WAYNE COUNTY HISTORICAL MUSEUM

CE – **Richmond**. (765) 962-5756. Admission. (September, second weekend)

TRAIL OF COURAGE LIVING HISTORY FESTIVAL

NC – **Rochester**, FCHS grounds four miles north of Rochester on US 31. **www.icss.net/~fchs/events.htm**. The Trail of Courage portrays history when northern Indiana was still Potawatomi territory, before the terrible forced removal of 1838, known as the Trail of Death. Each year the Trail of Courage honors a different Potawatomi family that had ancestors on the Trail of Death or signed treaties in Indiana. The public is invited to join in the Indian dances from 2 to 4 p.m., which are held in an arena encircled by teepees. This program of Indian dances is an educational exhibit, not a Pow Wow. There is also a recreation of Chippeway, the first trading post, post office and village in Fulton County in 1832. Canoe rides; muzzle loading shooting and tomahawk throwing contests, and a frontier blab school adds to the frontier activities. Admission. (third weekend in September)

BACK TO THE DAYS OF KOSCIUSZKO

NC – Warsaw. County 4H Fairgrounds. (574) 269-6803 or **www.backtothedays.com.** Admission. (third weekend in September)

HERITAGE FESTIVAL

NE – Berne. Swiss Heritage Village. (260) 589-8007 or **www.bernein.com/heritagedays.htm.** Pioneer games, storytelling, scarecrow contest, apple cider press, village tours, pioneer music and food, Native American dancing. Admission. (September, second weekend)

JOHNNY APPLESEED FESTIVAL

NE – Fort Wayne. Johnny Appleseed Park. (260) 497-6000. Celebrate the life and times of John Chapman. 100,000 attendance. Vendors and musicians wear period dress. FREE. (third weekend in September)

FORKS OF THE WABASH PIONEER FESTIVAL

NE – Huntington. Hiers Park. (800) 848-4282 or **http://pioneerfest.huntingtoncounty.org.** Admission. (third or fourth weekend in September)

STONE'S TRACE PIONEER FESTIVAL

NE – Ligonier. (888) 417-3562 or **www.stonestrace.com.** Pony cart rides, tour of Stone's Tavern, pioneer music, tomahawk throwing, circuit riding preacher, women's skillet throw, log splitting, primitive muzzle loading demos, food and entertainment. Admission. (weekend after Labor Day)

Pioneer Days / Encampments *(cont.)*

BUCKSKINNERS RENDEZVOUS

NW – Cutler. Adams Mill. (765) 463-7893. FREE. (last Saturday in Saturday)

DUNELAND HARVEST FESTIVAL

NW – Porter. Chellberg Farm & Bailly Homestead. (219) 926-7561. FREE. (third weekend in September)

OLD SETTLERS DAYS

SE – Salem. John Hays Center. (812) 883-4303. Storytelling, pioneer kids activities. FREE. (mid-month in September)

OCTOBER

CIVIL WAR DAYS & LIVING HISTORY

CE – Hartford City. SR 26E. www.hartfordcitycwdays.com. (765) 348-4319. Also tour a medical training school. Admission. (second weekend in October)

CANAL DAYS & TRADERS RENDEZVOUS

CE – Metamora. (765) 647-2194 or **www.metamora.com**. Little shops plus historical vendors and re-enactors. FREE. (first weekend in October)

PIONEER DAYS

CW – Terre Haute. Fowler Park Grist Mill area. (812) 462-3391. FREE. (first weekend in October)

FEAST OF THE HUNTER'S MOON

CW – West Lafayette. Fort Quiatenon Historic Park. South River Road. **www.tcha.mus.in.us/feast.htm**. (765) 476-8402. Re-creation of life at this 18th century French trading post. Admission. (first weekend in October)

MISSISSINEWA 1812

NC – **Marion**. Battlefield. **www.mississinews1812.com**. (800) 822-1812 or Largest War of 1812 living history event in the U.S. with average attendance of 30,000. Admission. (end of first full week of October)

APPLE FESTIVAL

NE – **Kendallville**, Noble County Fairgrounds. (260) 347-4035 or **www.kendallvilleapplefestival.com**. Pioneer festival highlights the years 1800-1865. Skill demonstrators, primitive area, entertainment, kid's activities, antiques, crafts, and foods. FREE. (first weekend in October)

BUCKLEY HOMESTEAD DAYS

NW – **Lowell**. (219) 696-0769. Admission. (first weekend in October)

AUTUMN ON THE RIVER

SE – **Bethlehem**. Town Commons. (812) 256-6111. Recreation of founding of Bethlehem in 1812. Taste this town's famous steamboat stew and flatboat bean soup. FREE. (third weekend in October)

FT. VALLONIA DAYS

SE – **Vallonia**. (888) 524-1914. Reconstructed fort/tepees. FREE (third weekend in October)

MUSTER AT WABASH BLUFFS

SW – **Vincennes**. Indiana Territory State Historic Site. (812) 882-7422. FREE. (end of October or early November weekend)

Master
Index

Activity Index

PROUDLY

MADE IN THE USA

Travel Journal & Notes:

Travel Journal & Notes:

Travel Journal & Notes:

_____
_____
_____
_____
_____
_____
_____
_____
_____
_____
_____
_____
_____
_____
_____
_____
_____
_____
_____
_____
_____
_____
_____
_____
_____
_____
_____
_____
_____
_____
_____
_____
_____

Travel Journal & Notes:

Travel Journal & Notes:

GROUP DISCOUNTS & FUNDRAISING OPPORTUNITIES!

We're excited to introduce our books to your group! These guides for parents, grandparents, teachers and visitors are great tools to help you discover hundreds of fun places to visit. Our titles are great resources for all the wonderful places to travel either locally or across the region.

We are two parents who have researched, written and published these books. We have spent thousands of hours collecting information and *personally traveled over 25,000 miles* visiting all of the most unique places listed in our guides. The books are kid-tested and the descriptions include great hints on what kids like best!

Please consider the following Group Purchase options: *For the latest information, visit our website:* **www.KidsLoveTravel.com**

❑ **Group Discount/Fundraising** – Purchase books at the discount price of $2.95 off the suggested retail price for members/friends. Minimum order is ten books. You may mix titles to reach the minimum order. Greater discounts (~35%) are available for fundraisers. Minimum order is thirty books. Call for details.

❑ **Available for Interview/Speaking** – The authors have a treasure bag full of souvenirs from favorite places. We'd love to share ideas on planning fun trips to take children while exploring your home state. The authors are available, by appointment, *(based on availability)* at (614) 792-6451 or **michele@kidslovepublications.com**. A modest honorarium or minimum group sale purchase will apply. Call or visit our website for details.

Call us soon at (614) 792-6451 to make arrangements!
Happy Exploring!

All titles are "Kid Tested". *The authors and kids personally visited all of the most unique places* and wrote the books with warmth and excitement from a parent's perspective. Listings provide: Names, addresses, telephone numbers, websites, directions, and descriptions. All books include a bonus chapter listing state-wide kid-friendly Seasonal & Special Events!

❏ **KIDS LOVE GEORGIA** - Explore hidden islands, humbling habitats, and historic gold mines. See playful puppets, dancing dolphins, and comical kangaroos. "Watch out" for cowboys, Indians, and swamp creatures. Over 500 listings in one book about Georgia travel. 6 geographical zones, 272 pages.

❏ **KIDS LOVE INDIANA** - Discover places where you can "co-star" in a cartoon or climb a giant sand dune. Over 500 listings in one book about Indiana travel. 8 geographical zones, 280 pages.

❏ **KIDS LOVE KENTUCKY** - Discover places from Boone to Burgoo, from Caves to Corvettes, and from Lincoln to the Lands of Horses. Nearly 500 listings in one book about Kentucky travel. 5 geographic zones. 186 pages.

❏ **KIDS LOVE MICHIGAN** - Discover places where you can "race" over giant sand dunes, climb aboard a lighthouse "ship", eat at the world's largest breakfast table, or watch yummy foods being made. Almost 600 listings in one book about Michigan travel. 8 geographical zones, 229 pages.

❏ **KIDS LOVE NORTH CAROLINA** - Explore places where you can "discover" gold and pirate history, explore castles and strange houses, or learn of the "lost colony" and Mayberry. Over 500 listings in one book about travel. 6 geographical zones, 280 pages.

❏ **KIDS LOVE OHIO** - Discover places like hidden castles and whistle factories. Over 800 listings in one book about Ohio travel. 9 geographical zones, 260 pages.

❏ **KIDS LOVE PENNSYLVANIA** - Explore places where you can "discover" oil and coal, meet Ben Franklin, or watch your favorite toys and delicious, fresh snacks being made. Over 900 listings in one book about Pennsylvania travel. 9 geographical zones, 268 pages.

❏ **KIDS LOVE TENNESSEE** – Explore places where you can "discover" pearls, ride the rails, "meet" Three Kings (of Rights, Rock & Soul). Be inspired to sing listening to the rich traditions of Country music fame. Over 500 listings in one book about Tennessee travel. 6 geographical zones, 235 pages.

❏ **KIDS LOVE THE VIRGINIAS** – Discover where ponies swim and dolphins dance, dig into archaeology and living history, or be dazzled by record-breaking and natural bridges. Over 900 listings in one book about Virginia & West Virginia travel. 8 geographical zones, 262 pages.

ORDER FORM

KIDS LOVE PUBLICATIONS

1985 Dina Court, Powell, Ohio 43065
(614) 792-6451
Visit our website: **www.KidsLoveTravel.com**

#	Title		Price	Total
	Kids Love Georgia		$14.95	
	Kids Love Indiana		$14.95	
	Kids Love Kentucky		$13.95	
	Kids Love Michigan		$13.95	
	Kids Love North Carolina		$14.95	
	Kids Love Ohio		$13.95	
	Kids Love Pennsylvania		$13.95	
	Kids Love Tennessee		$13.95	
	Kids Love the Virginias		$13.95	
	Kids Love Travel Memories!		$14.95	
	Combo Discount Pricing			
	Combo #2 - Any 2 Books		$26.95	
	Combo #3 - Any 3 Books		$37.95	
	Combo #4 - Any 4 Books		$47.95	
(Please make check or money order payable to: KIDS LOVE PUBLICATIONS)			**Subtotal**	
		(Ohio Residents Only – Your local rate)	Local/State Sales Tax	
☐ Master Card		*$2.00 first book $1.00 each additional*	Shipping	
☐ Visa			**TOTAL**	

Account Number ☐☐☐☐-☐☐☐☐-☐☐☐☐-☐☐☐☐

Exp Date: ☐☐/☐☐ (Month/Year)

Cardholder's Name _____

Signature *(required)* _____

Name: _____

Address:_____

City:_____State:_____

Zip:_____Telephone:_____

All orders are shipped within 2 business days of receipt by US Mail. If you wish to have your books autographed, please include a <u>legible</u> note with the message you'd like written in your book. Your satisfaction is 100% guaranteed or simply return your order for a prompt refund. Thanks for your order. Happy Exploring!

"Where to go?, What to do?, and How much will it cost?", are all questions that they have heard throughout the years from friends and family. These questions became the inspiration that motivated them to research, write and publish the "Kids Love" travel series.

This adventure of writing and publishing family travel books has taken them on a journey of experiences that they never could have imagined. They have appeared as guests on hundreds of radio and television shows, had featured articles in statewide newspapers and magazines, spoken to thousands of people at schools and conventions, and write monthly columns in many publications talking about "family friendly" places to travel.

George Zavatsky and Michele (Darrall) Zavatsky were raised in the Midwest and have lived in many different cities. They currently reside in a suburb of Columbus, Ohio. They feel very blessed to be able to create their own career that allows them to research, write and publish a series of best-selling kids' travel books. Besides the wonderful adventure of marriage, they place great importance on being loving parents to Jenny & Daniel.